Praise for

Reinventing Collapse

Orlov has a brilliant mind. This is a lucid thought experiment of what could happen to the United States in the event of collapse, whether caused by dependence on oil, debt, other deficits, or, simply, the complexity and fragility of the system. A must-read for all those who study fragility and risk management.

— NASSIM N. TALEB, Distinguished Professor of Risk Engineering, NYU-Poly, author *The Black Swan*

Dmitry Orlov brings a penetrating intelligence to a subject few dare to face squarely: the impending tragic implosion of the American Dream. He writes with assurance, clarity and wit from a singular point-of-view – someone who has witnessed the prior Soviet crack-up. This book is indispensable for anyone who seeks to understand the economic storm that is about to make landfall on our shores.

— JAMES HOWARD KUNSTLER, author *The Long Emergency*

Dmitry Orlov is a genius. *Reinventing Collapse* in its original version has more than stood the test of time and events as a prophetic vision of the challenges that are being so clearly defined for us as a civilization today. The new and revised edition is priceless because it incorporates current events and emerging trends and views them through the eyes of this terrific writer and thinker. And Orlov's sense of humor always plants a minefield full of laugh bombs in the right places. Nobody sees it like Orlov and nobody says it like Orlov.

— MICHAEL C. RUPPERT, author *Crossing the Rubicon*

Be prepared to have your window shoved open and feel the fresh air shake you up. But don't worry, reading Dmitry Orlov usually just means gaining special insights with a strange, humorous twist. Dmitry is unique, contributing mightily to the vital but suppressed discussion of collapse and rebirth.

— JAN LUNDBERG, Culture Change

Unlike many commentators, Orlov has seen collapse first hand, in the Former Soviet Union — there aren't too many books about the impending collapse of civilization that make you laugh out loud, but *Reinventing Collapse* is one of them.

— BART ANDERSON, energybulletin.net

Heretical, hysterically funny, always on point, deeply perceptive – Dmitry Orlov has been through a societal collapse and come out the other side. On that other side is a fascinating view of contemporary American society, a good deal of wisdom and a surprising amount of hope – not that some magical transformation will fix everything for us, but that even the collapse of empire is not the end of the world.

— SHARON ASTYK, author *Depletion & Abundance: Life on the New Home Front* and blogger, www.sharonastyk.com

Orlov's Russian perspective on the American collapse is valuable not just for its predictions, but for its attitude: economic collapse is not an unthinkable horror, but a routine and fascinating part of history, and if you find yourself in one, you should look around.

— RAN PRIEUR, ranprieur.com

Dmitry Orlov has set out to write a gloomy comparison of what happened to Russia at the end of the Soviet Empire and how ill-prepared the American Empire is for the same fate, and ended up writing something wickedly funny, profoundly hopeful and filled with good advice. His advice is not to avoid collapse, that would be futile, but to prosper and thrive in the midst of it.

— ALBERT BATES, attorney, inventor, and author *The Post-Petroleum Survival Guide and Cookbook*

Reinventing Collapse

The Soviet Experience
and American Prospects

Revised and Updated

Dmitry Orlov

NEW SOCIETY PUBLISHERS

Cover design by Diane McIntosh. Illustration: copyright © Hyun Jung Lee

Printed in Canada. First printing March 2011.

Paperback ISBN: 978-0-86571-685-8
eISBN: 978-1-55092-475-6

Inquiries regarding requests to reprint all or part of *Reinventing Collapse* should be addressed to New Society Publishers at the address below.

To order directly from the publishers, please call toll-free (North America) 1-800-567-6772, or order online at www.newsociety.com

Any other inquiries can be directed by mail to:

New Society Publishers
P.O. Box 189, Gabriola Island, BC V0R 1X0, Canada
(250) 247-9737

Library and Archives Canada Cataloguing in Publication

Orlov, Dmitry
    Reinventing collapse : the Soviet exerience and American prospects / Dmitry Orlov. -- Rev. and updated

Includes index.
ISBN 978-0-86571-685-8

    1. Economic forecasting--United States. 2. United States--Economic condtions--2009-. 3. United States--Economic conditions--2001-2009. 4. United States--Politics and government--2001-2009. 5. Soviet Union--History--1985-1991. I. Title.

HC106.83.O75 2011   330.973093   C2011-900658-8

New Society Publishers' mission is to publish books that contribute in fundamental ways to building an ecologically sustainable and just society, and to do so with the least possible impact on the environment, in a manner that models this vision. We are committed to doing this not just through education, but through action. Our printed, bound books are printed on Forest Stewardship Council-certified acid-free paper that is **100% post-consumer recycled** (100% old growth forest-free), processed chlorine free, and printed with vegetable-based, low-VOC inks, with covers produced using FSC-certified stock. New Society also works to reduce its carbon footprint, and purchases carbon offsets based on an annual audit to ensure a carbon neutral footprint. For further information, or to browse our full list of books and purchase securely, visit our website at: www.newsociety.com

NEW SOCIETY PUBLISHERS

Mixed Sources
Cert no. SW-COC-001271
© 1996 FSC

Contents

Join the Conversation

Visit our online book club at www.newsociety.com
to share your thoughts about *Reinventing Collapse*.
Exchange ideas with other readers, post questions for the author,
respond to one of the sample questions or start
your own discussion topics. See you there!

Preface to Second Edition

THE BOOK YOU SEE BEFORE YOU WAS WRITTEN between 2005 and 2007 and first published in the spring of 2008. The study and observations that went into writing it spanned a longer period: from 1989 to 2006. In this book I had made a number of predictions, many of which have since started to come true. Now, in 2010, the idea of the US going the way of the USSR is no longer quite so controversial: "Don't worry about using the term 'collapse' — that's the term they are using at the White House" a senior Washington insider told me recently. In many ways, collapse is already here; it just hasn't been widely distributed yet.

While updating the text for the second edition, I have been careful not to add any new predictions, but I did take a few out because, as I now realize, energy and financial trends are too volatile to call over as short a term as the publication cycle of a book. Global oil production appears to have peaked for good, but is yet to start seriously declining, and this has produced a slow-motion crash rather than an outright collapse. Financially, the high volume of debts going bad has so far outpaced the government's printing presses, keeping inflation out of the picture, while creative accounting at the Federal Reserve has so far prevented a run on the US dollar, though how long this can continue is anyone's guess. We are in uncharted territory; all we know is that there is a cliff up ahead.

This book compresses a significant period of time into a single, foreshortened historical episode: the collapse of the two late-20th-century superpowers. Some day it may be distilled into just one chapter of a history textbook — one that will talk about the long-gone USSR and the long-gone USA. Schoolchildren will like learning about the superpowers just as they like learning about dinosaurs: big, scary monsters — but extinct, and therefore not so frightening. The following chapter might talk about the end of the industrial age, with pictures of other impressive dinosaurs: offshore oil and gas platforms and refineries; supertankers, bulk carriers, container ships and aircraft carriers; giant office towers and big box stores surrounded by vast wastelands of parking lot and freeway; megaschools, megafactories and megahospitals and other industrial megafauna from the late Anthropocene. To future schoolchildren, these pictures will look as exotic as Mayan pyramids or Mesopotamian ziggurats. But I am getting ahead of myself.

The schoolchildren of the future aside, this book might be able to help us, here and now, with our own perception of time as it relates to large-scale changes. We tend to believe that the present is well known, but that the future can only be guessed at by extrapolating charts and graphs and formulating alternative scenarios at various levels of probability. We tend to discount the probability of sweeping changes, choosing to believe instead that the future will resemble the present. In doing so, we may be correct up to 99 percent of the time; the rest of the time we get it so completely wrong as to look utterly ridiculous. What's more, that 1 percent shows up every 100 times or so. The future doesn't so much unfold as dawn on us one fine morning.

Sometimes the arrival of this realization can be distilled down to a single moment. When I visited Russia in the summer of 1989, nobody was talking about the collapse of the USSR. Getting ready to go back again a year later, I had to delay my trip in order to get my infected appendix excised. Going under the knife at Brigham and Women's Hospital, I was chatting with the surgeon while the anesthesiologist was getting ready to pump me full of sodium pentathol. The surgeon was interested in what was going to become of the Soviet socialist republics, Armenia in particular. Right before I winked out and he got busy slicing and dicing, I rather surprised myself by assuring him that

Armenia would become independent within a year, and I recall him looking a bit incredulous. Armenian independence came on September 21, 1991.

It is helpful to be able to recognize the imminent arrival of major changes before most other people, with one important caveat: enough other people have to be able to recognize them too — once you point them out. If not, then your destination may well turn out to be the loony bin. When I came back from a visit to Russia in 1996, I was quite certain that the USA was going to go the way of the USSR, although I wasn't sure about the timing. But I realized that few people would agree with me, and so I kept my findings to myself until 2005, when I correctly surmised that a critical mass of people would be open to considering them. I started paying attention to Peak Oil theory at around the same time, but its timing remained uncertain, and the theory, sound though it seemed, remained consigned to the heretical fringe. Then Peak Oil showed up in the aggregate oil production statistics, in 2005 for conventional oil and in 2008 for all liquid fuels. More importantly, the effects of Peak Oil contributed to the massive spike in oil prices, which was one of the causative factors in the ensuing financial collapse. So now I feel confident that, once I point it out, many people will recognize one important but generally unrecognized flaw in Peak Oil theory, as it stands, which I point out for the first time in this edition, in the section on energy.

When confronting a reasonably successful prognosticator such as myself, the obvious question to ask is, How did he know? Sadly, there isn't any point of technique I can share with the world. It's a matter of recognizing an element of the future when it shows up within our notional "present." But such recognition is not a conscious, rational process. We never know how we knew. If pressed, we come up with justifications of how we knew, which upon examination turn out to be contrived. What makes recognition possible is the ability to see patterns based on the sum total of our life experiences, not some analytical ability or access to data. I am certain that watching one superpower collapse has primed me to recognize, ahead of most other people, those same telltale tendencies in the other. A certain amount of perspective also seems necessary: I was able to observe the Soviet collapse over a series of visits, and this gave my observations a time-lapse effect. I am sure that I would not have been able to make the same observations had I been living there at the time, stuck in the moment, with all my energies devoted to mere survival.

Another prerequisite is a bit of detachment: I refuse to become emotional or sentimental about collapse. My life is my own, and, may superpowers fall where they may, I will try to live it as best I can. I hope that by keeping this book alive I can help others do the same.

Boston, New England
September 2010

Introduction

I AM NOT AN EXPERT or a scholar or an activist. I am more of an eyewitness. I watched the Soviet Union collapse and this has given me the necessary insights to describe what the American collapse will look like. It has been a couple of years since I started writing on the subject of economic collapse as it occurred in the Soviet Union and as it is likely to occur here in the United States. Thus far, I remain reasonably content with my predictions: all the pieces of the collapse scenario I imagined are lining up, slowly but surely.

But for me it all started late in the summer of 1996, when I arrived in the US after an extended stay in Russia. I was just married and my thoughts turned to the future. I had visited Russia many times before, on family visits as well as on business trips, and had been able to observe in detail the fall of Communism and the ensuing economic collapse. Unlike the people who had lived there throughout that period, and also unlike those who had visited just once or twice, I was able to notice both the gradual changes and the sudden ones. Because I was born and grew up in Russia, I was not thwarted by any cultural or linguistic barriers. It was just the place where I grew up, in some ways remarkably unchanged after more than a decade of absence, but in other ways remarkably transformed.

By the time my wife and I settled back in the States, I had seen and heard enough to grasp the complete and utter hollowness of bombastic phrases such as "the defeat of Communism" or "Cold War victory." For a time, there was even talk of the Cold War paying a dividend, but it was soon followed by recriminations over "who lost Russia." I had already understood that the Soviet collapse had precious little to do with Communist ideology, and was not hugely influenced by anything Americans said or did. Rather, I could not help but feel that the relative timing of the collapse of the two superpower adversaries was a matter of luck. And so I came back to the States expecting that the second superpower shoe would be dropping sometime soon, certainly within my lifetime, and the question for me became: How soon?

Let us imagine that collapsing a modern military-industrial super-power is like making soup: chop up some ingredients, apply heat and stir. The ingredients I like to put in my superpower collapse soup are: a severe and chronic shortfall in the production of crude oil (that magic addictive elixir of industrial economies), a severe and worsening foreign trade deficit, a runaway military budget and ballooning foreign debt. The heat and agitation can be provided most efficaciously by a humiliating military defeat and widespread fear of a looming catastrophe. In the Soviet case, crude oil production peaked a few years before the collapse, foreign trade imbalance had much to do with the Soviets' inability to grow enough food or manufacture enough consumer goods, the military budget was huge to start with and was further swelled by the Soviets' knee-jerk response to a silly thing called "Star Wars," Afghanistan provided the military humiliation and Chernobyl the backdrop of catastrophe.

It took a couple of decades for the United States to catch up, but now all the ingredients are in the pot and starting to simmer. US crude oil production peaked in 1970 and global (conventional) crude oil production appears to have peaked sometime in 2005, with all of the largest oil fields in terminal decline and global oil exports set to start crashing. The trade imbalance is such that the US produces little of the high technology on which it depends, having exported jobs and moved production offshore for over a generation now. Although the US grows enough food to feed itself, it imports the fossil fuels with which to grow it and deliver it, at a ratio of roughly nine calories of fossil fuels to one calorie of food. The runaway military budget, which now stands at one trillion dollars a year, has been swelled by something called the "War on Terror." The situation with regard to runaway foreign debt is slightly different: it is denominated in America's own currency, giving the US the option of inflating it away rather than defaulting on its obligations. But the results are the same: a worthless national currency and unhappy international creditors unwilling to extend further credit. Iraq provides the needed military defeat and killer hurricanes that are part of global climate upheaval the fear of a catastrophe.

Let us not even try to imagine that this will all just blow over. Make no mistake about it: this soup will be served, and it will not be tasty! My soup-based method of predicting superpower collapse may not please a scholar or an expert or an activist (as I mentioned, I am none of these) but it is probably rigorous enough to adequately warn and equip an innocent bystander. I am not too interested in constructing rigorous scientific models and producing forecasts. Nor do I wish to set agendas, promote reforms or take part in protests. Try to form a picture in your mind: it is a superpower, it is huge, it is powerful, and it is going to come crashing down. You or me trying to do something about it would have the same effect as you or me wiggling our toes at a tsunami. Nor do I wish to force my opinions on you, so please form your own. But I do want to guide your imagination by providing a lot of real world detail about an actual economic collapse that has recently transpired, along with some honest, apples-to-apples, oranges-to-oranges comparisons between the United States and the Soviet Union, to serve as a foundation for setting some commonsense expectations and making your own plans, separately from the happy toe-wiggling masses.

People generally find it hard to act on knowledge that contradicts their everyday experience. The experience must come first, even if it is second-hand; hence all the support groups for people who want to change their lives or their habits. There are plenty of books on subjects similar to this one, complete with tables of figures, charts, graphs and diagrams, that argue for or against this or that thesis, initiative or proposal. This, I hope you will be happy to find, is not one of them. My goal is to take various important aspects of the Soviet post-collapse experience and to recast them in an American context, allowing you to imagine what will become of your surroundings, your situation and your options. I hope to add a lot of detail to what, I would hazard to guess, is currently something of a white spot on your cognitive map. In the same way that medieval cartographers sometimes drew sea monsters on yet-to-be-explored sections of the ocean, perhaps yours is populated by dreary Mel Gibson clones, or leather-clad extras from the movie *Waterworld*, or those charming little Cannibalistic Humanoid Underground Dwellers from *C.H.U.D.*, Douglas Cheek's 1984 film in which grotesquely deformed sewer dwellers terrorize New York.

Beyond giving your imagination something meaty to chew on, I would like you to take some specific steps, but it would be arrogant of me to presume to know what they should be. You will have to work that out for yourself. Here is one starting point: currently, over a third of the working-age population in the United States responds in the negative to the survey question "Will you be able to afford to retire?" Perhaps you are one of them or would consider joining them after giving the question some thought. By the way, the question is splendidly euphemistic, making it seem as if being ready for retirement is like being ready for the big weekend. The actual question is, "Will you be able to survive once you are too old to work?" If not, then what are you planning to do about it? Slave away until destitute old age catches up with you? Here is a bad solution: get drunk a lot. With any luck, you would not live long enough to reach retirement age and you would be too drunk to care even if you did. I don't wish to set any unreasonable expectations, but I do hope that I can help you come up with a better solution than that!

Let's keep in mind that in every age and circumstance, some people have always managed to find enlightenment, fulfillment and freedom: this is the best that can be hoped for. And I hope that by helping you overcome your fear of the future and the old, ingrained habits of thought that promote reliance on what must surely be a transient and unstable present, I will make it easier for you to start your process of adaptation sooner than necessary, instead of too late, and to go on to live a full and happy life, come what may.

The Soviet Example

A DECADE AND A HALF AGO the world went from bipolar to unipolar, because one of the poles fell apart: The SU is no more. The other pole — symmetrically named the US — has not fallen apart, yet; but there are ominous rumblings on the horizon. The collapse of the United States seems about as unlikely now as the collapse of the Soviet Union seemed in 1985. The experience of the first collapse may be instructive to those who wish to survive the second.

I anticipate that some Americans will react rather badly to having their country compared to the USSR. I would like to assure you that the Soviet people would have reacted similarly, had the United States collapsed first. "Of course the United States collapsed," they would have said, "and why wouldn't it have? It was a hopelessly backward system, destined for the scrapheap of history: self-enriching political elites, industry predicated on generating profits for the elites rather than on serving public needs, boom and bust cycles, homelessness, unemployment, a legacy of slavery and Indian genocide, yadda-yadda. What could it possibly have in common with us, who solved all these problems decades ago, thanks to progressive social policy and centrally planned production? Stop prattling on about that failed former British colony! We have more important things to do than listen to you! We are busy building Communism — on Mars!"

Jingoism, you see, is usually a two-sided coin, neither side containing anything particularly informative. Feelings aside, here are two 20th century superpowers, who wanted more or less the same things — things like technological progress, economic growth, full employment and world domination — but disagreed about the methods. And they obtained similar results — each had a good run, intimidated the whole planet and kept the other scared. Each eventually went bankrupt.

Reasonable people would never argue that the two poles were exactly symmetrical; along with significant similarities, there are equally significant differences. Both are valuable in predicting how the second half of the clay-footed superpower giant that once bestrode the planet will fare once it too falls apart. Until recently, however, few people would have taken this premise seriously. After all, who could have doubted that the world economic powerhouse that is the United States, having recently won the Cold War and the Gulf War, would continue, triumphantly, into the bright future of superhighways, supersonic jets and interplanetary colonies? But more recently the number of doubters has started to climb steadily.

One key observation is that the US economy is dependent on the availability of cheap, plentiful oil and natural gas to a greater extent than any other country. Once oil and gas become expensive (as they already have) and in ever-shorter supply (a matter of one or two years at most), economic growth will stop and the economy will collapse. The term "collapse" as I try to use it here has been given a precise meaning by John Michael Greer's theory of catabolic collapse in his 2005 book *How Civilizations Fall: A Theory of Catabolic Collapse.* According to this theory, collapse can be calculated to occur when "production fails to meet maintenance requirements for existing capital." The theory adds some much needed rigor to the poorly understood recurring phenomenon of advanced societies suddenly going "poof."

But even without delving too deeply into theory, it is possible to sketch out very simple collapse scenarios that anyone can understand. Oil powers just about everything in the US economy, from food production and distribution to shipping, construction and plastics manufacturing. When less oil becomes available, less can be produced, and economic growth comes to an end. In an economy that is designed to operate at a steady state this would not be such a problem, but the US economy operates on debt, and the value of debt is based on the promise of future growth. Without growth, debt pyramids begin to crumble, and once that happens, less money is available for such things as oil imports. Lather, rinse, repeat. A while later, look around: Where did that economy disappear to?

At this point, it appears that 2005 set the all-time record in global (conventional) oil production and although it is still theoretically possible that this record will be exceeded in coming years, pessimistic, and usually under-reported, news of rapidly depleting reserves, delayed projects and collapsing production at key supergiant fields far outweighs optimistic, and usually over-hyped, news of new discoveries or new projects coming on-stream. There is also a cottage industry of professional optimists, proudly serving the needs of clients whose long-term investment strategy is to continually invest for the short term. Optimism is contagious, and so they are the ones who get most of the press.

Not that the professional realists are in short supply. They are to be found at the CIA, the Defense Department, the General Accounting Office and the US Congress. They all insist that looming energy shortages are a severe threat and that something must be done to address them. (The most realistic of these realists point out that something should have been done about it already, starting one or two decades ago.) More and more municipalities across the country are passing Peak Oil resolutions, determined to cut energy consumption before circumstances force their hand. Efforts to label the observable, measurable phenomenon of peaking oil production as a "theory" neatly parallel the efforts of global warming deniers. Note, however, that what is known on the subject now is more or less what was known a decade or so ago. Thus, the lack of attention paid to it over the decades resulted not from ignorance but from denial: although the basic theory that is used to model and predict resource depletion has been well understood since the 1960s, most people prefer to remain in denial. And although the dynamics of denial are a bit off the subject of Soviet collapse and what it may teach us about our own, I can't resist saying a few words about it, for it is such an interesting subject. I also hope that it will help some of you to go beyond denial, this being a helpful step towards understanding what I am going to say here.

Now that a lot of the Peak Oil predictions are coming true more or less on schedule, and it is becoming increasingly difficult to ignore the steady climb of energy prices and the dire warnings from energy experts of every stripe, outright denial is being gradually replaced with subtler forms of denial, which center around avoiding any serious, down-to-earth discussion of the likely actual consequences of Peak Oil and the ways one might cope with them.

Instead, there is much discussion of policy: what "we" should do. The "we" in question is presumably some embodiment of the Great American Can-Do Spirit: a brilliantly organized consortium of government agencies, leading universities and research centers and major corporations, all working together toward the goal of providing plentiful, clean, environmentally safe energy to fuel another century of economic expansion. Welcome to the sideshow at the end of the universe!

One often hears that "We could get this done, if only we wanted to." Most often one hears this from non-specialists, sometimes from economists, but hardly ever from scientists or engineers. A few back-of-the-envelope calculations are generally enough to suggest otherwise, but here logic runs up against faith in the Goddess of Technology: that she will provide. On her altar are assembled various ritualistic objects used to summon the Can-Do Spirit: a photovoltaic cell, a fuel cell, a vial of ethanol and a vial of bio-diesel. Off to the side of the altar is a Pandora's box packed with coal, tar sand, oceanic hydrates and plutonium: if the Goddess gets angry, it's curtains for life on Earth.

But let us look beyond mere faith, and focus on something slightly more rational instead. This "we," this highly organized, high-powered problem-solving entity, is quickly running out of energy, and once it does, it will not be so high-powered any more. I would like to humbly suggest that any long-term plan it attempts to undertake is doomed, simply because crisis conditions will make long-term planning, along with large, ambitious projects, impossible. Thus, I would suggest against waiting around for some miracle device to put under the hood of every SUV and in the basement of every McMansion, so that all can live happily ever after in this suburban dream, which is looking more and more like a nightmare in any case.

The next circle of denial revolves around what must inevitably come to pass if the Goddess of Technology were to fail us: a series of wars over ever more scarce resources. Paul C. Roberts, who is very well informed on the subject of Peak Oil, has this to say: "What desperate states have always done when resources turn scarce ... [is] fight for them." (*Mother Jones*, November 12, 2004) Let us not argue that this has never happened, but did it ever amount to anything more than a futile gesture of desperation? Wars take resources; when resources are already scarce, fighting wars over resources becomes a lethal exercise in futility. Those with more resources would be expected to win. I am not arguing that wars over resources will not occur. I am suggesting that they will be futile, and that victory in these conflicts will be barely distinguishable from defeat. I would also like to suggest that these conflicts would be self-limiting: modern warfare uses up prodigious amounts of energy, and if the conflicts are over oil and gas installations, then they will get blown up, as has happened repeatedly in Iraq. This will result in less energy being available and, consequently, less warfare.

Take, for example, the last two US involvements in Iraq. In each case, as a result of US actions Iraqi oil production decreased. It now appears that the whole strategy is a failure. Supporting Saddam, then fighting Saddam, then imposing sanctions on Saddam, then finally overthrowing him, has left Iraqi oil fields so badly damaged that the "ultimate recoverable" estimate for Iraqi oil is now down to 10–12 percent of what was once thought to be underground (according to the *New York Times*).

Some people are even suggesting a war over resources with a nuclear endgame. On this point, I am optimistic. As Robert McNamara once thought, nuclear weapons are too difficult to use. And although he has done a great deal of work to make them easier to use, and had considerable success in advocating the introduction of small, tactical, battlefield nukes and the like, and despite recently renewed interest in nuclear "bunker busters," they still make a bit of a mess and are hard to work into any sort of a sensible strategy that would reliably lead to an increased supply of energy. Noting that conventional weapons have not been effective in this area, it is unclear why nuclear weapons would produce better results.

But these are all details; the point I really want to make is that proposing resource wars, even as a worst-case scenario, is still a form of denial. The implicit assumption is this: if all else fails, we will go to war; we will win; the oil will flow again; and we will be back to business as usual in no time. Again, the Iraqi experience should be enough to sober up anyone still waiting around for the success of a global police action to redirect the lion's share of the dwindling world oil supplies toward the United States.

Outside this last circle of denial lies a vast wilderness called the Collapse of Western Civilization, roamed by the Four Horsemen of the Apocalypse, or so some people will have you believe. Here we find not denial but escapism: a hankering for a grand finale, a heroic final chapter. Civilizations do collapse — this is one of the best-known facts about them — but as anyone who has read *The Decline and Fall of the Roman Empire* will tell you, the process can take many centuries.

What tends to collapse rather suddenly — and with far greater regularity than civilizations — is the economy. An economy does not collapse into a black hole from which no light can escape. Instead, something else happens: society begins to spontaneously reconfigure itself, establish new relationships and evolve new rules, in order to find a point of equilibrium at a lower rate of resource expenditure.

Note that the exercise carries a high human cost: without an economy, many people suddenly find themselves as helpless as newborn babes. Many of them die sooner than they would otherwise: some would call this a "die-off." There is a part of the population that is most vulnerable: the young, the old and the infirm; the foolish and the suicidal. There is also another part of the population that can survive indefinitely on insects and tree bark. Most people fall somewhere in between.

Economic collapse gives rise to new, smaller and poorer economies. That pattern has been repeated many times, so we can reason inductively about similarities and differences between a collapse that has already occurred and one that is about to occur. Unlike astrophysicists, who can confidently predict whether a given star will collapse into a neutron star or a black hole based on measurements and calculations, we have to work with general observations and anecdotal evidence. However, I hope that my thought experiment will allow me to guess correctly at the general shape of the new economy, and arrive at survival strategies that may be of use to individuals and small communities.

The Collapse of the Soviet Union: An Overview

What happens when a modern economy collapses and the complex society it supports disintegrates? A look at a country that has recently undergone such an experience can be most educational. We are lucky enough to have such an example in the Soviet Union. I spent about six months living, traveling and doing business in Russia during the *perestroika* period and immediately afterward, and was fascinated by the transformation I witnessed.

The specifics are different, of course. The Soviet problems seem to have been largely organizational rather than physical in nature, although the fact that the Soviet Union collapsed just three years after reaching peak oil production is hardly a coincidence. The ultimate cause of the Soviet Union's spontaneous collapse remains shrouded in mystery. Was it Ronald Reagan's Star Wars? Or was it Raisa Gorbachev's American Express card? It is possible to fake a missile defense shield; it is not so easy to fake a Harrods department store. The arguments go back and forth. One contemporary theory would have it that the Soviet elite scuttled the whole program when they decided that Soviet Socialism was not going to make them rich. (It remains unclear why it should have taken the Soviet elite 70 years to come to this startlingly obvious conclusion.)

A slightly more commonsense explanation is this: during the pre-*perestroika* "stagnation" period, due to the chronic underperformance of the economy, coupled with record levels of military expenditure, trade deficit and foreign debt, it became increasingly difficult for the average Russian middle-class family of three, with both parents working, to make ends meet. (Now, isn't that beginning to sound familiar?) Of course, the government bureaucrats were not too concerned about the plight of the people. But the people found ways to survive by circumventing government controls in a myriad of ways, preventing the government from getting the results it needed to keep the system going. Therefore, the system had to be reformed. When this became the consensus view, reformers lined up to try and reform the system. Alas, the system could not be reformed. Instead of adapting, it fell apart.

Russia was able to bounce back economically because it remains fairly rich in oil and very rich in natural gas, and will probably continue in relative prosperity for at least a few more decades. In North America, on the other hand, oil production peaked in the early 1970s and has been in decline ever since, while natural gas production is now set to fall off a production cliff, notwithstanding the recent desperate and environmentally destructive use of "Fracking" to get at shale gas. Yet energy demand continues to rise far above what the continent can supply, making such a spontaneous recovery unlikely. When I say that Russia bounced back, I am not trying to understate the human cost of the Soviet collapse or the lopsidedness and the economic disparities of the reborn Russian economy. But I am suggesting that where Russia bounced back because it was not fully spent, the United States will be more fully spent and less capable of bouncing back.

But such "big picture" differences are not so interesting. It is the micro-scale similarities that offer interesting practical lessons on how small groups of individuals can successfully cope with economic and social collapse. And that is where the post-Soviet experience offers a multitude of useful lessons.

Back in the USSR

I first flew back to Leningrad, which was soon to be rechristened St. Petersburg, in the summer of 1989, about a year after Gorbachev freed the last batch of political prisoners, my uncle among them, who had been locked up by General Secretary Andropov's final, senile attempt at clenching an iron fist. For the first time it became possible for Soviet escapees to go back and visit. More than a decade had passed since I left, but the place was much as I remembered it: bustling streets full of Volgas and Ladas, Communist slogans on the roofs of towering buildings lit up in neon, long lines in shops.

About the only thing new was a flurry of activity around a newly organized Cooperative movement. A newly hatched entrepreneurial class was busy complaining that their "cooperatives" were only allowed to sell to the government, at government prices, while they contrived ingenuous schemes to skim something off the top through barter arrangements. Most were going bankrupt. It did not turn out to be a successful business model for them or for the government, which was, as it turned out, also on its last legs.

I went back a year later and found a place I did not quite recognize. First of all, it smelled different: the smog was gone. The factories had largely shut down, there was very little traffic and the fresh air smelled wonderful! The shops were largely empty (in the sense of being quite uncontaminated by consumer goods) and often closed. There were very few gas stations open and the ones that were had lines that stretched for many blocks. There was a ten-liter limit on gasoline purchases.

Since there was nothing better for us to do, my friends and I decided to take a road trip to visit the medieval Russian cities of Pskov and Novgorod, taking in the surrounding countryside along the way. For this, we had to obtain fuel. It was hard to come by. It was available on the black market, but no one felt particularly inclined to let go of something so valuable in exchange for something so useless as money. Soviet money ceased to have value, since there was so little that could be bought with it, and people still felt skittish around foreign currency.

Luckily, there was a limited supply of another sort of currency available to us. It was close to the end of Gorbachev's ill-fated anti-alcoholism campaign, during which vodka was rationed. There was a death in my family, for which we received a funeral's worth of vodka coupons, which we of course redeemed right away. What was left of the vodka was placed in the trunk of the trusty old Lada, and off we went. Each half-liter bottle of vodka was exchanged for ten liters of gasoline, giving vodka far greater effective energy density than rocket fuel.

When the time came for the trip back, we discovered that we definitely did not have enough gas. Worse yet, we were out of vodka! I was doing my usual meander through closed gas stations and empty industrial back lots, questing after gasoline, idling in third gear and trying not to touch either the gas pedal or the brakes to conserve the precious vapors. Finally, I spotted my quarry: a plucky urchin with a jerrycan. I was sent in to negotiate. Knowing how little we had to offer, I worked hard to establish understanding, sympathy and trust. This took some time. After a while, it did appear that we would get some gas, but not without parting with something valuable. The plucky urchin wanted a replacement for his unfashionable sweatpants and his imagination inevitably seized upon the jeans I was wearing. We were considering a trade, but then even he conceded that I would look ridiculous in his sweatpants. The deal remained tentative all the while the gasoline was being dispensed, but in the end he walked away, disappointed, with just a wad of rubles. To celebrate, we stopped for a picnic in a forest. Back on the highway, as we approached the hillside studded with giant concrete letters spelling "Leningrad Region," our urchin friend was perched on top of the letter "L," his jerrycan by his side. Had I brought a spare pair of jeans, we could have obtained a reserve; without it, we crawled back into town timidly, with hardly a slosh to be heard from the gas tank, and his wardrobe remained unfashionable.

There is a lesson to be learned here: when faced with a collapsing economy, one should stop thinking of wealth in terms of money. Access to actual physical resources and assets, as well as intangibles such as connections and relationships, quickly becomes much more valuable than mere cash.

A Rude Awakening

Two years later, I was back again, this time in the dead of winter. I was traveling on business through Minsk, St. Petersburg and Moscow. My mission was to see whether any of the former Soviet defense industry could be converted to civilian use. I toured formerly top secret factories and institutes. I managed to get a sample batch of product (little circuit boards) shipped to the US, but only after the government delayed the shipment and slapped on an export duty that neatly equaled our margin on the entire production run. So, the business part of the trip was a total fiasco and a complete waste of time, just as one would expect. In other ways, it was quite educational.

Minsk seemed like a city rudely awakened from hibernation. During the short daylight hours, the streets were full of people, who just stood around as if wondering what to do next. The same feeling pervaded the executive offices, where people I used to think of as the representatives of the "evil empire" sat around under dusty portraits of Lenin bemoaning their fate. No one had any answers.

The only beam of sunshine came from a smarmy New York lawyer who hung around the place trying to organize a state lottery. He was almost the only man with a plan. The director of a research institute which was formerly charged with explosion-welding parts for nuclear fusion reactor vessels also had a plan: he wanted to build summer cottages. The director of another research institute, one formerly charged with developing the silent magneto-hydrodynamic drive for nuclear submarines, had taken to hunting ducks in the city park. He proudly reported them to be free of radionuclides, but they tasted quite vile. There were also a lot of German businessmen, ostensibly in town on business, but really just to drink on the cheap and to sample the local women, a wide assortment of whom was on display at each of the two big tourist hotels.

I wrapped up my business early and caught a night train to St. Petersburg. On the train, a comfortable old sleeper car, I shared a compartment with a young, newly retired army doctor, who explained to me a truly medieval technique of curing recruits of the common cold using a vat of hot water and some turpentine, showed me his fat roll of hundred-dollar bills, and told me all about the local diamond trade. He was also dabbling in real estate: apartments in St. Petersburg were then selling for around one twenty-fifth of what they are worth now. We split a bottle of cognac and snoozed off. It was a pleasant trip.

St. Petersburg was a shock. There was a sense of despair that hung in the winter air. There were old women standing around in spontaneous open-air flea markets trying to sell toys that probably belonged to their grandchildren to buy something to eat. Middle-class people could be seen digging around in the trash. Everyone's savings had been wiped out by hyperinflation. I arrived with a large stack of one-dollar bills. Everything was one dollar, or a thousand rubles, which was about five times the average monthly salary. I handed out lots of these silly thousand-ruble notes: "Here, I just want to make sure you have enough." People would recoil in shock: "That's a lot of money!" "No, it isn't. Be sure to spend it right away." However, all the lights were on, there was heat in many of the homes and the trains ran on time.

My business itinerary involved a trip to the countryside to tour and have meetings at a scientific facility. The phone lines to the place were down, and so I decided to just jump on a train and go there. The only train left at 7 a.m. I showed up around 6, thinking I could find breakfast at the station. The station was dark and locked. Across the street, there was a store selling coffee, with a line that wrapped around the block. There was also an old woman in front of the store, selling buns from a tray. I offered her a thousand-ruble note. "Don't throw your money around!" she said. I offered to buy her entire tray. "What are the other people going to eat?" she asked. I went and stood in line for the cashier, presented my thousand-ruble note, got a pile of useless change and a receipt, presented the receipt at the counter, collected a glass of warm brown liquid, drank it, returned the glass, paid the old woman, got my sweet bun, and thanked her very much. It was a lesson in civility. After that, there was nothing to do except stand on the dark platform, look at the one illuminated object — the clock — and wait for the train.

Once on the train, it eventually dawned on me that I didn't know where I should be getting off or where I should be going after that, so I strolled through the train, hoping to spot a scientist, I suppose. I found one fellow reading an English textbook and, considering it to be close enough, asked him whether he knew of the place I was visiting. Not only did he know it, but he worked there and knew the people I was planning to visit. We arrived there together, at what was clearly the most important building on the entire compound — the cafeteria — just as the lunch hour ended. Everyone felt sorry that I had missed lunch, but nothing could be done about it: lunchtime was officially over. This was quite an illustrious institution, with many world-renowned scientists who had contributed to international scientific collaborations, but it could no longer pay salaries, with the cafeteria remaining as one of the few remaining perks.

The New Normal

Three years later I was back again, and the economy had clearly started to recover, at least to the extent that goods were available to those who had money, but enterprises were continuing to shut down and most people were still clearly suffering. There were new, private shops, which had tight security, and which sold imported goods for foreign currency. Very few people could afford to shop at them. There were also open air markets in many city squares, at which most of the shopping was done. Many kinds of goods were dispensed from locked metal booths, quite a few of which belonged to the Chechen mafia: one shoved a large pile of paper money through a hole and was handed back the item. It was all a bit sketchy, but here, at least, one could pay with rubles.

There were sporadic difficulties with the money supply. I recall standing around waiting for banks to open in order to cash my traveler's checks. The banks were closed because they were fresh out of money; they were all waiting for cash to be delivered. Once in a while, a bank manager would come out and make an announcement: the money is on its way, no need to worry.

There was a great divide between those who were unemployed, underemployed or working in the old economy, and the new merchant class. For those working for the old state-owned enterprises — schools, hospitals, the railways, the telephone exchanges and what remained of the rest of the Soviet economy — it was lean times. Salaries were paid sporadically or not at all. Even when people got their money, it was barely enough to subsist on.

But the worst of it was clearly over. A new economic reality had taken hold. A large segment of the population saw its standard of living reduced, sometimes permanently. It took the economy ten years to get back to its pre-collapse level, and the recovery was uneven. Alongside the nouveaux riches, there were many whose fortunes would never recover. Those who could not become part of the new economy, especially the pensioners, but also many others who had benefited from the now defunct socialist state, could barely eke out a living.

This thumbnail sketch of my experiences in Russia is intended to convey a general sense of what I had witnessed. But it is the details of what I have observed that I hope will be of value to those who see an economic collapse looming ahead and want to plan in order to survive it.

My Premise

You may have guessed by now that an economic collapse is amazing to observe, and very interesting if described accurately and in detail. A general description tends to fall short of the mark, but let me try. An economic arrangement can continue for quite some time after it becomes untenable, through sheer inertia. But at some point a tide of broken promises and invalidated assumptions sweeps it all out to sea.

One such untenable arrangement — the one on which continued US prosperity currently rests — assumes that it is possible to perpetually borrow more and more money from abroad to pay for more and more energy imports, while the price of these imports continues to double every few years. Free money with which to buy energy equals free energy, and free energy does not occur in nature. This must therefore be a transient condition. When the flow of energy snaps back toward equilibrium, much of the US economy will quite literally run out of fuel, and will be forced to shut down. This is but one such untenable arrangement; there are many others as well.

I therefore take it as my premise that at some point during the coming years, due to an array of factors, with energy scarcity foremost among them, the economic system of the United States will teeter and fall, to be replaced by something that most people can scarcely guess at, and that even those who see it coming prefer not to think about. This stunning failure of the collective imagination is the specific problem this book seeks to address.

The risk is there for all to see, and it is huge. Even if you happen to believe that the probability of economic collapse is low, it is the product of the two — the probability of it happening times the value of everything that is at risk — against which you should seek to insure yourself. In a nation that insures itself against loss of life and limb, car accidents, medical emergencies, fire, flood, accidents at sea and pratfalls resulting in litigation, such wanton disregard is most striking.

Perhaps it is difficult for a people that attempt to quantify every kind of risk in terms of its monetary value to think about a type of risk that can only be compensated for through accepting a different living arrangement. Perhaps it is difficult for a nation that has not experienced war on its home soil in many generations to imagine a future that does not generally resemble the past. Americans still appear to see theirs as the land of free ice cream and perpetual sunshine — much evidence to the contrary — in a way that the Russians or the Germans or the Chinese decidedly do not. Or perhaps the force of the social convention that a modicum of optimism be required for one's admission into polite company throws up an invisible perceptual barrier.

Perhaps most importantly, America's national mythology makes it anathema to think of collective failure. All failure is to be regarded as individual failure — something that happens to somebody else, or to you, but only if you happen to be unlucky or do not try hard enough. Fair enough: economic collapse will in fact happen for each of you individually, in turn. For some, like the retired schoolteacher in Santa Barbara who lives in a car with her cats, it has happened already. Certain others will have to wait their turn, until one day they find that the mansion is cold and dark, the Rolls Royce is out of gas, and the bank is out of money, so there is nothing left to do except mix really stiff drinks and sit around the fireplace.

Whatever the causes of this failure of collective imagination happen to be, I believe I have found a way to break down this wall. My method is one of comparative analysis, taking the actual pre- and post-collapse conditions in the Soviet Union and comparing them to the hypothetical pre- and post-collapse conditions in the United States. I will focus on categories that are key for survival: food, shelter, transportation, education, finances, security and a few others. In general, whether post-collapse conditions for each of these categories are dire or relatively benign depends in great measure on how closely coupled the pre-collapse arrangement is to the smooth functioning of the rest of the economic system. Looking at each of these factors in turn will help focus the imagination on the salient details of each thing, rather than the vague big picture.

Then, of each important thing in your life, you will be prepared to answer two very important questions: "Is it collapse-proof? " and, if it is not, "What can I do to make it collapse-proof? " If, for a given thing, the answers turn out to be "No" and "Nothing," then the very important follow-up question should be: "How can I live without it?"

Having obtained these answers, it will be up to you whether to act on them and how quickly. It takes a brave and independent nature to follow your own orders, rather than try to fulfill the expectations of the people around you. And it will take imagination and actual work, as well as a good deal of luck, to adequately collapse-proof yourself and your family.

But even if the steps you take are largely symbolic, their value as mental preparation will not be. An economic collapse is the worst possible time to suffer a nervous breakdown, yet so often this is exactly what happens. Taking an unsentimental look at what is coming up can help put you at the top of your game at a time when everyone around you is reeling in shock and flailing about randomly. This will make you a very useful person, both to yourself and to others, in making the best of a bad situation. This is also something that you and I should realistically expect to be able to achieve.

Superpower Similarities

O FFICIAL PROPAGANDA has always tried to portray superpower conflict as an obvious and inevitable consequence of the irreconcilable differences between the two sides. One's own side was represented as the manifestation of all that is good and just in the world and the other as all that is evil and repressive. There was usually a catchy label to go with the description that tested well with the target audience, such as the "Imperialist Aggressor" or the "Evil Empire." When you switched sides, the orientation of the propaganda you had just heard flipped automatically: it was like stepping through a mirror.

It is axiomatic that in order for a contest to make an engaging spectacle, the contestants have to be evenly matched. A mock pugilistic contest between a schoolgirl and her pet kangaroo may provide amusement, but it cannot be regarded as proper sport. What we generally look for is a fair fight, or at least the semblance of one, and this requires that the two fighters weigh about the same, have similar training and be able to go on expertly punching and blocking for several rounds. They would probably turn out to have other things in common as well: a diet rich in red meat or a tendency to try solving many different kinds of problems by throwing punches. A given audience may decide to cheer one and boo the other, making the contest more interesting to watch, but that is irrelevant to the outcome.

If a contest goes on for an extended period of time — in the case of the superpower contest, over three decades — it would appear safe to conclude that the contestants had been evenly matched. But we will probably never know for certain why the Soviet fighter chose to take a dive in the fourth round, because that certainly did not look like a proper knockout. It is also hard to understand why the American fighter concluded his little victory jig by kneeing himself in the teeth, or why he is now draped unconscious over the ropes and getting pummeled by some junior featherweights from the stands. And why is the Soviet fighter now seated back in his corner, laughing? It is never easy to give up the title of World Superpower Champion, especially when it is not being challenged, but this is ridiculous! What sort of sporting event is this anyway? Bring back the schoolgirl and the kangaroo!

Turning slightly more serious, some would find a direct comparison between the United States and the Soviet Union incongruous, if not downright insulting. After all, what grounds are there to compare a failed Communist empire to the undisputed world leader? Others might find it preposterous that the loser might have advice for the winner in what they might see as an ideological conflict. Since the differences between the two appear glaring to most, let me just indicate some similarities, which I hope you will find are no less obvious.

The Soviet Union and the United States are each either the winner or the runner-up in the following categories: the space race, the arms race, the jails race, the hated evil empire race, the squandering of natural resources race and the bankruptcy race. In some of these categories, the United States is, shall we say, a late bloomer, setting new records after its rival was forced to forfeit. Both believed, with giddy zeal, in science, technology and progress, right up until the Chernobyl disaster occurred. After that, there was only one true believer left.

They are the two post-World War II industrial empires that attempted to impose their ideologies on the rest of the world: democracy and capitalism versus socialism and central planning. Both had some successes: while the United States reveled in growth and prosperity, the

Soviet Union achieved universal literacy, universal health care, far less social inequality and a guaranteed — albeit lower — standard of living for all citizens. The state-controlled media took pains to make sure that most people didn't realize just how much lower it was: "Those happy Russians don't know how badly they live," Simone Signoret said after a visit.

Both empires made a big mess of quite a few other countries, each one financing, funneling arms and directly taking part in bloody conflicts around the world in order to impose its ideology and thwart the other. Both made quite a big mess of their own country, setting world records for the percentage of population held in jails (South Africa was a contender at one point). In this last category, the US is now a runaway success, supporting a burgeoning, partially privatized prison-industrial complex.

While the United States used to have far more goodwill around the world than the Soviet Union, the "evil empire" gap has narrowed since the Soviet Union disappeared from the scene. Now, in many countries around the world, including Western countries like Sweden, the United States ranks as a bigger threat to peace than Iran or North Korea. In the hated-empire race, the United States is now beginning to look like the champion. These almost universal negative feelings are likely to prove more durable than the superpower's good fortune: nobody likes a loser, especially if the loser is a failed superpower. Nobody had any pity for the poor defunct Soviet Union, and nobody will have any pity for poor defunct America either.

The bankruptcy race is particularly interesting. Prior to its collapse, the Soviet Union was taking on foreign debt at a rate that could not be sustained. The combination of low world oil prices and a peak in Soviet oil production sealed its fate. Later, the Russian Federation, which inherited the Soviet foreign debt, was forced to default on its obligations, precipitating an international financial crisis. Russia's finances later improved, primarily due to rising oil prices along with rising oil exports, and it is now well on its way to becoming an energy superpower.

The United States is now facing a current account deficit that cannot be sustained, a falling currency and an energy crisis, all at once. It is now the world's largest debtor nation, and most people do not see how it can avoid defaulting on its debt. According to a lot of analysts, it is technically bankrupt and is being propped up by foreign reserve banks, which hold a lot of dollar-denominated assets and, for the time being, want to protect the value of their reserves. This game can only go on for so long. Thus, while the Soviet Union deserves honorable mention for going bankrupt first, the gold in this category (pun intended) will undoubtedly go to the United States, for the largest default ever.

There are many other similarities. For instance, both countries have been experiencing chronic depopulation of farming districts. In Russia, family farms were decimated during collectivization, along with agricultural output; in the US, a variety of other forces produced a similar result with regard to rural population, but without any loss of production. Both countries replaced family farms with unsustainable, ecologically disastrous industrial agribusiness, addicted to fossil fuels. The American ones work better, as long as energy is cheap and, after that, probably won't work at all.

All the similarities are too numerous to mention. I hope that what I outlined above is enough to signal a key fact: that these are, or were, the antipodes of the same industrial, technological civilization. But what is interesting for our purposes is to identify and describe the key elements that made these superpower contestants so evenly matched that their sparring went on for decades.

None of these key elements can be sustained forever. The hypothesis I wish to test is that the lack of these same key elements, readily identifiable in the Soviet collapse, likewise spells the demise of America, definitely as a superpower, probably as a major part of the world economy, and possibly as a recognizable entity on the political map.

The Myth of Inclusiveness

Like that of our metaphorical heavyweight champion, a superpower's diet must contain plenty of red meat — in this case, human flesh. A superpower must continually ingest plenty of highly skilled and motivated personnel — managers, scientists, engineers, military officers — who must be willing to endure hardship, give up their best years, ruin their health, perhaps even give their lives, slaving away designing and building things, fighting and doing all the dirty work. Motivating the needed quantities of people with money is out of the question, because that would not leave enough for the ruling elites to siphon off. The upper classes tend to already be highly motivated by both money and status, but they also tend to be allergic to dirty work, and they can never be numerous enough to satisfy a superpower's appetite for flesh. The only thing that can possibly provide the necessary motivating force is an idea: a communal myth powerful enough to cause people to commit their insignificant yet essential selves to the righteousness and glory of the great whole. A superpower's vitality is critically dependent on the sustaining power of this myth. Shortly after it fails, so does the superpower.

Both the Soviet and the American models featured an inclusiveness myth as their centerpiece. In the Soviet case, it was the myth of the classless society. The great revolutionary upheaval was said to have erased class and ethnic distinctions, creating an egalitarian society that provided for everybody's basic needs, curbed excesses of wealth and allowed people from humble origins to become educated and rise to positions of respect and authority. This myth proved to be so powerful that it propelled a poor, industrializing but still mainly agrarian nation on a trajectory to becoming a leading military and industrial power. As the decades wore on, the myth gradually lost most of its luster. The satisfaction of basic needs gave rise to an insatiable appetite for imported consumer goods, which were either inaccessible or in short supply, except to the elite, and this, in turn, ruined the appearance of egalitarianism. "They pretend to pay us, and we pretend to work," went the saying, and morale plummeted. This led to a situation where no new common effort could be organized. As everyone started thinking for themselves, a slow rot set in, and the superpower gradually became enfeebled.

America's belated and half-hearted answer to the classless society of the Soviets is the middle class society. After wallowing through the Great Depression and grasping at straws during the New Deal, the United States reaped a gigantic windfall following World War II, as the only large industrial player left standing. Much of the rest of the world's industrial infrastructure had been bombed to rubble, giving the United States an opening. They used it to put every American within striking distance of achieving a cheap simulacrum of landed gentry, symbolized by a detached house surrounded by a patch of land big enough to accommodate private parking, a patch of grass and some shrubbery, and adorned, as an absolute necessity, by one's own private automobile. American society is classless, at least in theory, since no one wants to admit to being either upper or lower class. There is, supposedly, one large and homogeneous middle class; in fact, though, it has a small upper portion and a large and rapidly expanding lower portion.

The wonderful thing about the American middle class concept is its malleability, because it is almost entirely symbolic. You could be middle class, own an ancestral mansion in an old brick and fieldstone suburb, drive a Mercedes and send your children to an Ivy League school. Or you could be middle class, live in a dolled-up trailer home, drive a souped-up pickup truck and send your children to a community college that teaches them how to milk hogs. The least common denominator is that you have to drive a motor vehicle, otherwise you can no longer perform this charade.

This is why there is so much denial about it being necessary to give up the car and all the current talk about resorting to biofuels to continue feeding the car addiction. Biofuels amount to burning one's food and destroying what is left of the topsoil in order to continue driving. This is also why so many Americans would forgo a healthy diet, a reasonable work schedule, education for their children, needed medical treatment and even give up their house, rather than give up their car. Not having a car makes one, within the American suburban landscape, a non-person.

The universal right to drive a car is the linchpin of the American communal myth. Once a significant portion of the population finds that cars have become inaccessible to them, the effect on the national psyche may be so profound as to make the country ungovernable. Solving the underlying transportation problem, through the reintroduction of public transportation or other means, is beside the point: the image of the automobile is indelibly imprinted on the national psyche and it will not be easily dislodged. For many, their car is a public extension of their persona, a status symbol and even a symbol of sexual potency, and this makes the automobile, along with the gun, a sacred national fetish. Like the gun, the car is also a potent weapon that can be used for murder or for suicide. It is propelling the American communal myth toward a flaming crash with the reality of permanent fuel shortage, compared to which the gradual fading away of the Soviet communal myth will have been gentle and benign.

Better Living through Science

Both the United States and the Soviet Union aspired to achieving better living through science, staking their very existence on the ability to deliver technological fixes to all manner of existing problems, as well as to all the unforeseen new problems that were created in the course of applying technological fixes to existing problems. The inability to either prevent or successfully mitigate catastrophes, which, in a technology-based civilization, shows up as the inability to deal with a set of technical challenges, eventually destroys the population's faith in the system. In a society where every kind of prestige and status emanates from the exercise of technical prowess, such failure destroys trust and undermines respect for every kind of authority.

Each of the two superpowers strove to position itself at the forefront of science and technology. It is no surprise, therefore, that science and technology were arenas of serious competition and relentless copying between the superpowers. Americans led in product design; many Soviet research institutes were busy secretly reverse-engineering American-designed products. The Soviets held an advantage in basic science; numerous American PhD candidates laboriously deciphered the Cyrillic of obscure Soviet scientific articles, then scurried back to the lab to reproduce their results. Both superpowers produced impressive results in areas such as energy, power generation, weaponry, shipbuilding and aerospace. Soviet-built capital equipment has proven to be extremely hardwearing and relatively easy to maintain, and Soviet-built motor vehicles, aircraft and plenty of other machinery are still in use throughout Eastern Europe, Africa and Asia. In an ironic twist, Soviet-built planes have been pressed into service to resupply

American troops in Iraq and Afghanistan because they are uniquely able to handle rutted and cratered runways.

One area of superpower technology competition that was particularly bound up with national prestige was the space race. The two early Russian wins — the first unmanned success of the Sputnik, and Yuri Gagarin's first manned orbital flight — struck fear into the hearts of Americans, causing them to get slightly more serious about learning math and Russian and in due course to counter with the Apollo missions to the moon and other impressive exploits. The Soviet manned space program is alive and well under Russian management and now offers first-ever space charters. (As I write this, a former Microsoft executive is on his way to the International Space Station, accompanied by two Russian cosmonauts, having paid $20 million for the privilege. Once there, he will try making some of Dr. Martha Stewart's cookie recipes in zero gravity — important scientific work, to be sure!) Americans from the official space program have been hitching rides on the Soyuz as well, while most of their remaining spaceships sat in the shop, plagued by loose heat tiles and cracks in the foam insulation, before finally being retired with nothing to replace them. To be fair, the Americans have been quite successful with their unmanned missions to Mars, fly-by missions to the outer planets and other robotic spacecraft.

The Soviet Union failed to remain technologically competitive in three important technological categories: food production, consumer goods and information technology. None of these factors was lethal on its own, but the combination was quite damaging, to the prestige as well as the pocketbook. It is uncanny that the United States now appears poised to fail in these same categories as well — which is why I chose to include them here.

Industrial Food Production

There is no reason why food production should be relegated to the area of technology; after all, people grew and gathered food with little or no technology for many thousands of years. But the introduction of collectivized, mechanized agriculture broke the back of pre-revolutionary Russian agrarian society, and no amount of technical supervision from Moscow was able to restore the prolific productivity of the backward old village.

In most parts of Russia, agriculture has always been a somewhat dubious proposition. The growing season is short. The soils are thin outside of a single belt of fertile black soil called *chernozëm* that runs through Ukraine and some of Russia's southern regions. There are frequent spring droughts and early cold snaps. These factors make very marginal yields and outright failed harvests quite common, and there have been several episodes of outright starvation. Because agriculture is so unreliable, throughout their long history Russians have augmented it with other types of traditional economic activity (so-called *promysly*) such as fur trapping, hunting, fishing and logging. Nevertheless, before the havoc wreaked by World War I and the ensuing revolution, Russia was by all accounts a well-fed country, known for its blini-eating contests, that supplied wheat to Western Europe. In Soviet times, it had to import wheat from the United States and Canada on credit, and many people were forced to supplement what was available in the state-run shops with what they could buy at the farmers' markets, gather in the woods and produce from their own small kitchen garden plots.

Corporate, mechanized agriculture in the United States is often viewed as a success story, able to supply its people with a high-fat, high-protein diet, which also contains plenty of salt and sugar, along with many mystery chemicals. Never mind that it spans the entire spectrum of flavors — from sawdust all the way to cardboard — cleverly disguised by the fat, salt, sugar and mystery chemicals. Never mind that this questionable food is often ingested in a hurry, from a piece of paper or plastic. Never mind that it makes the people fat, crazy and sick. The portions are nothing if not generous, even for the poorest people, many of whom sport cathedral-like domes and buttresses of fat.

The US also produces many agricultural commodities for export. However, this agricultural system depends on the availability of fossil fuel-based energy, mainly in the form of diesel for agricultural machinery and transportation and natural gas for fertilizer and other chemical manufacturing. In effect, the industrialized agricultural system transforms fossil fuels into food calories with the help of soil (which it gradually destroys in the process) and sunlight. The ratio of fossil fuel energy to derived food energy has been calculated to be about ten calories from fossil fuels for each calorie of consumed food. The combination of depleted domestic oil and gas resources and demand outstripping foreign supplies, coupled with increasing demand for biofuels and the predicted onset of dust-bowl conditions due to global warming, represents a less than rosy scenario for American food security in the coming years.

Consumer Goods

The Soviets' inability to compete in the area of mass-produced consumer goods stemmed mainly from an administrative preference for financing capital goods expenditures while ignoring light industry. Also, consumer goods production requires a flexible economic model that is difficult to accommodate within a centrally planned economy. Consumer goods were regarded not as an important segment of the Soviet economic system but as a cost to the government, competing with other, more essential social services such as housing, education and health care. As it turned out, the trickle of imported consumer items eventually turned into a flood; coupled with falling oil export revenues, this exacerbated the Soviet Union's financial shortfalls.

Since the talent to design fashionable, attractive clothing was certainly always present, this was strictly a failure — one of many — on the part of the Soviet leadership. What they entirely missed was the ability of consumer goods, especially clothing, to undermine morale by allowing privileged young people to differentiate themselves in appearance from the rest of the population, and to do so in a way that quietly made a mockery of the official ideology, without any sign of overt dissent. It is well known that putting on a uniform has a profound effect on a person's behavior. Attire that is branded with an ideologically charged symbol actually influences one's ideology, because putting it on implies making a statement, and because people tend to agree with themselves, standing by the statements they make. Consequently, putting on attire that is branded with an ideologically hollow symbol, such as a designer logo, is a way of shrugging off ideology altogether and of denying the power of ideologically charged symbols. It gave young people a painless way to opt out of looking and feeling Soviet.

Today, the United States is being flooded with imported consumer goods, just as the Soviet Union was during the stagnation period of the '80s, and with similar impact on the country's trade deficits, but here these branded products are too common to serve as a social differentiator. To the contrary, with the exception of sports brands, it is the cheap clothing that is most often emblazoned with a corporate brand, not the high-priced articles. The few consumer articles that are still manufactured in the United States more often than not have a strangely old-fashioned, stolid, institutional look, reminiscent of Soviet production, and maintain their tentative foothold within the domestic market by appealing to the US consumer's sense of patriotism. When the exporting countries finally decide to stop selling their products on credit, and their container ships stop visiting America's ports, perhaps the institutional look will become fashionable. Then again, the homemade look may win out, or the threadbare look, or the clothing-optional look; the future of fashion is hard to predict. The worst possible outcome is that everyone will don uniforms, fashioning themselves into identical, mass-produced, ideologically lobotomized servants of the fully privatized, corporate-run state.

Information Technology

One area of superpower competition in which the United States declared early victory, and in which it is now handily defeating itself, is the area of information technology. The Soviet Union failed to keep up for a number of reasons, but perhaps the most important one was the insistence that the whole endeavor be shrouded in secrecy, for security reasons, due to the Soviet government's deep mistrust of its own people. Their failure to keep up was especially striking in view of the fact that they had some of the best talent. During the late '70s, many of the pioneering American computer companies were staffed by specialists who had recently emigrated from Russia.

Also, the explosive development of computer technology has generally proceeded through oversight and random, accidental successes, rather than through successful central planning. The US funded the development of Internet routing protocols hoping to create a network that would be resilient in the face of nuclear attack. Luckily, this ability was never to be tested, but the factors that made it resilient also made it anarchic, and this eventually gave us worms and viruses, botnets, peer-to-peer networks and spam. IBM released their PC architecture into the wild, thinking it worthless, and others took the basic blueprint and made a multitude of cheap clones of it. A few tinkerers in a garage came up with the first generation of Apple's machines. A few other tinkerers at Bell Labs used their copious spare time to write the Unix operating system, more or less as a joke, and it eventually took over most of the bigger machines. It later morphed into Linux, which is now gradually taking over many of the smaller ones. Microsoft blundered across a good thing when IBM mistakenly failed to provide a viable operating system for the PC, and no amount of subsequent blundering has been able to erase this initial advantage. The Soviets, with their secretiveness and tight central control, simply could not match this level of amateurism, haphazard innovation and random improvisation.

It took a while, but the United States eventually found ways to approximate the Soviet failure in this area, and is presently hard at work looking for creative ways to kill the goose that lays golden eggs — by developing some secretiveness and tight central control of its own. The US is executing a three-pronged attack on the goose: through enforcing intellectual property laws, through criminalizing work in the area of computer security and through perpetuating a fraud called enterprise software, which has become something of a poster child for national dysfunction.

It is in the nature of all information to want to spread freely, and networked computers make it ridiculously easy for it to do so. This is really just a minor effect, because information found ways to be shared before the advent of computers and it will go on being shared after the lights go out for good and the disk drives stop spinning. But as computers started to displace newspapers, stereos, television sets and library books, corporate interests decided to start charging rent on the use of information, as opposed to charging for products or services, and they pushed through laws to make that possible. These laws are hard to enforce and the information they are intended to hold for ransom is easy to liberate, with some unintended consequences. It is now possible to buy a DVD of an American film — or any other — in Beijing or Moscow before it even premieres in the United States. It also means that a Chinese or a Russian can generally use any commercial software free of charge, whereas an American has to either pay for it or be threatened with prosecution. The officials in these countries actually like intellectual property laws, because they give them arbitrary authority to prosecute anyone they happen to dislike, but, based on their record of enforcing these laws, they seem to like most people. Finally, let us consider the fact that American corporate equity, with intellectual property included, is being bought up by foreign interests, which are no longer happy accepting US Treasury paper. What this means, in the end, is that Americans will be reduced to paying foreigners for the privilege of using their own creations, while everyone else enjoys them free of charge.

Add to this the dubious American innovation of extending patent law to cover software. Software is basically speech — an expression of the programmer's thoughts in mathematical or logical constructs — and software patents are limits on such speech, restricting what sorts of things a programmer is allowed to write. According to the very highly respected computer scientist Donald Knuth, the computer revolution of the 1980s would probably never have happened had software patents existed then. The existence of software patents means that any software project may run afoul of some number of patents, which are expressed in vague and tortured legalese, making it legally unsafe to sell software in the United States without entering into various corporate alliances and cross-licensing agreements. The only viable strategy with regard to software patents is to fashion yourself into a sufficiently large nuisance by having plenty of patents of your own and by threatening litigation against anyone who infringes on them, so that anyone thinking of litigating against you would opt to negotiate a cross-licensing arrangement instead. This strategy is only open to large and well-connected software companies, because all the smaller ones would be automatically bankrupted by the exorbitant costs of litigation. Historically, these large companies are also the ones that are the least likely to do innovative work.

This is not to imply that software patents are beneficial even for the software giants. For them, the software patent system is like a large wrecking ball swinging about the software industry, toppling this or that part of it. A recent example is the pending lawsuit filed by Oracle Corporation against Google, based on patents Oracle came to own as a result of acquiring Sun Microsystems. The irony of the situation is that many of the patents in question are essentially nuisance patents, filed by Sun's engineers as a defensive measure after they had lost a patent infringement lawsuit filed by IBM. Sun lost, essentially, because it didn't hold enough patents at the time. One of the key patents held by IBM and infringed upon by Sun — the so-called "RISC patent" — basically said, once you strip away all of the ridiculous legalese, that if you make a microprocessor simpler, it will run faster. One of the patents Sun filed in response (by none other than James Gosling, the father of the Java programming language) basically describes a software analogue of using a light switch to control a light bulb. You see, Sun's engineers were competing to see just how ridiculous a software patent can be and still be granted by the patent office. The definitive answer is that the sky is the limit. The first software patent ever granted was the proverbial lawyer's nose under the tent.

With regard to computer security, the United States is making strides in making its computers less secure. Computer systems are considered secure if they are very difficult to break into (it is never impossible, unless the power is off or the network cable is unplugged) and not by virtue of the fact that nobody is trying to break into them. In fact, if the general public is prevented from even trying, then we are to assume that they are not secure at all, because they have not been tested in a real world environment. For many years now federal prosecutors in the United States have been generating consternation and outrage in England and beyond by trying to extradite a troubled British youth, Gary McKinnon, who broke into some Department of Defense systems looking for evidence of UFOs. Clearly, American officials find it easier to secure their jails than their computer systems, but since it is not possible to preemptively imprison every potential hacker, this is not an effective workaround. Such prosecutorial zeal is very helpful to professional information thieves, who might want to hack into the government's systems in order to accomplish something more serious — say, steal a nuclear bomb or two — by making sure that their security remains untested by helpful amateurs.

The third prong of the three-pronged attack on IT is the effort to maximally bureaucratize the process of software development via something called enterprise software. The programmer is now buried under layers of non-programmers: product managers, project managers, solutions architects, various other managers and directors, and let's not forget marketing and sales. The product, if one ever emerges, is evaluated by technical buyers, not by the poor people who will have to actually use it. The software itself is built up of a multitude of pieces, many of them purchased and licensed separately, and getting these pieces to talk to each other often requires diplomatic efforts by a team of consultants.

Finally, it all has to be written in a language that is maximally bureaucratized as well. Imagine a language whose dictionary defines each noun as a list of other nouns, which are defined elsewhere, followed by a list of verbs that apply specifically to that noun, but only some of which are defined. Now try writing something meaningful in this language. You will have to be creative, because you will have to find ways to navigate the strictures of the language, but you will soon enough find that you are too demoralized to actually say anything new or interesting. Is it any wonder, then, that so few people want to get degrees in computer science? And so it happens that all the best software is now written outside of the large software companies and is free, while horribly bloated, bug-infested, expensive, unstable and only marginally usable software is more often than not the flagship product of one of America's premier software companies. Information technology is one of the few sectors of the economy that the United States could be proud of, and these developments do not bode well for it.

The Cost of Technological Progress

Whether one succeeds or fails in any given technological endeavor, technological progress itself exacts a high cost on both the natural and the man-made environment. Both in the former Soviet Union and in North America, the landscape has fallen victim to a massive, centrally managed uglification program. Moscow's central planners put up identical drab and soulless buildings throughout the vastness of Soviet territory, disregarding regional architectural traditions and erasing local culture. America's land developers have played a largely similar role, with a similarly ghastly result: the United States of Generica, where many places can be told apart only by reading their highway signs. The commonplace result is a place not worth caring about — whether you are from there or not, it is just like most other such places in the world.

The Soviet public's faith in science and technology was severely shaken by the explosion of nuclear reactor number four at Chernobyl. Not only did the disaster itself expose an obvious lack of technical competence (it was caused, it later turned out, by the technical incompetence of some political appointees), but the lack of truthfulness in addressing the immediate consequences and in communicating the true state of affairs to the public did much to undermine trust in the government, as well as tarnishing the prestige of science and technology overall. Initial public pronouncements that "the reactor core is being cooled" were followed by evidence that there was no reactor core left. Highly radioactive chunks of nuclear fuel and graphite moderator rods that once made up the reactor core were later found scattered around the reactor site. The catastrophe awakened a latent environmentalist sentiment within the population: these were their ancestral lands that were being made radioactive and uninhabitable for generations. Specialists with access to scientific equipment ceased to have faith in the veracity of official government research and began to make and exchange their own measurements of radioactivity and industrial pollutant levels. The results were not encouraging and many started to feel that the Soviet economic development program had to be shut down.

Until 2010, America's answer to the Chernobyl disaster had been the handling of the humanitarian disaster following Hurricane Katrina in 2005. In 2010, it managed to do one better in the aftermath of the blowout, explosion and massive oil spill at BP's Deepwater Horizon offshore drilling platform in the Gulf of Mexico. The similarities between Katrina and Chernobyl included a lack of truthfulness in addressing the immediate consequences, loss of ancestral lands and political appointeeism (a horse specialist nicknamed "Brownie" was thrust in command, based on his credentials as the college roommate of a friend of the President). After the hurricane, the government continued to claim that the refugees were being evacuated, while in reality they were herded together, turned back by police and national guard troops when they tried to walk out of the disaster zone and allowed to die. As with Chernobyl, the government continued to lie until there was a public outcry, with much damage to the reputations of all concerned.

With the Deepwater Horizon disaster, the analogy with Chernobyl is much more direct, because both events fall into the category of technogenic catastrophes — direct failures of technology — rather than natural disasters. After Chernobyl, Soviet nuclear power stations were retrofitted with safety equipment that has so far prevented another disaster. It is not at all certain that a similar approach can be applied to deepwater drilling because of the already extremely high costs of these operations. Technology which can and sometimes does fail catastrophically, causing unacceptable levels of environmental devastation, but which cannot be retired for economic reasons, amounts to a false choice between physical survival and economic survival.

True to pattern, just as after Katrina, there followed an impressive display of official mendacity, fecklessness and shenanigans. Highlights included a video of retired coast guard admiral Thad Allen declaring that the well has been plugged in the attempted "top kill" operation appearing on news web sites right next to a live webcam of the selfsame well, gushing just as before. A truly astounding feature of BP's spill mitigation strategy was to *disperse* the oil (by spraying massive amounts of the toxic dispersant Corexit into the sea) while simultaneously attempting to *contain* the oil, both at the seafloor and at the surface. Just as you'd expect, dispersal precludes containment. As soon as the well was tentatively cemented shut, the White House rushed to announce that most of the leaked oil had somehow miraculously vanished — in fact, most of the spill has now taken the form of a giant deep underwater plume that stretches for miles and consists of a diffuse suspension of oil droplets. It will remain like this for years, drifting slowly, poisoning the marine food chain of the Gulf and the Atlantic waters beyond.

It remains to be seen which type of catastrophe predominates: natural or technogenic. On the one hand, increasingly frequent killer hurricanes and other extreme weather events, a predicted consequence of ongoing rapid climate change, are likely to repeat the Katrina pattern. On the other hand, now that all the easily-accessed offshore oil fields have been depleted, deepwater exploration and production will continue to become more challenging and more costly. One of the reasons the Deepwater Horizon exploded was that BP tried to drill the world's deepest oil well, but to do it on the cheap. The relentless pressure to cut costs is not conducive to improved safety, raising the probability of more giant explosions and massive oil leaks. Given the anemic response of the American political establishment to either of these disasters, this is more likely to be death by a thousand cuts. After each catastrophe, the promise of a technological remedy will begin to seem ever more outlandish, and the person proffering it will come to be seen as progressively less trustworthy. As the authorities lose their legitimacy in the eyes of the population, they will also lose its cooperation.

Militarism

The arms race is commonly viewed as the key element of the superpower standoff known as the Cold War (one hesitates to call it a conflict or even a confrontation because both sides diligently practiced conflict avoidance through deterrence, détente and arms control negotiations). Military deterrence and parity is seen as the paramount defining factor of the bipolar world that was dominated by the two superpowers. Military primacy between the United States and the Soviet Union was never actively contested and there was quite a lot of inconclusive militaristic preening and posturing. While the Americans feel that they won the Cold War (since the other side forfeited the contest) and were at one point ready to start awarding themselves medals for this feat, it is actually something of a success story for Russia.

Beyond the superficial and assumed offensive parity, the historical landscapes that underlie Soviet and American militarisms could not be more different. The United States considers itself a victor country: it goes to war when it wishes and it likes to win. It has not been invaded during any of the major modern conflicts and war, to it, is primarily about victory. Russia is a victim country. It has been invaded several times, but, since the Mongol invasion, never successfully. To Russians, war is not about victory — it is about death. The epithet that Russians like to apply to their country is *nepobedimaya* — "undefeatable."

The United States is a country that enjoys bombing other countries. The Soviets, having seen much of their country bombed to smithereens during World War II, had a particularly well-developed sense of their own vulnerability. To compensate for this, they devoted a large part of their centrally planned economy to defense. They produced a staggering number of nuclear missiles, nuclear submarines, tanks, bombers, fighter jets, warships and other military junk, much of which now sits quietly rusting somewhere, perpetually threatening to wreak havoc on the environment. The nuclear stockpile continues to pose a particularly nasty problem. Much of this war production was a complete waste and even the object of some humor: "I work at a sewing machine factory, but every time I bring the parts home and assemble them, I end up with a machine gun!" But they did not get bombed by the Americans — hence victory.

The list of countries which the US has bombed since the end of World War II is a long one, from "A" for Afghanistan to "Y" for Yemen (that the list does not run "A" to "Z" is presumably explained by the fact that Zambia and Zimbabwe do not present a sufficiently target-rich environment to America's military planners). The Soviet Union did not do nearly as much bombing. Czechoslovakia and Hungary received what amounted to a slap. Afghanistan was the one significant exception, playing host to a sustained and bloody military confrontation. Perhaps one positive effect of having one's homeland extensively bombed is that it makes one think twice about inflicting that experience on others.

And so it is quite a satisfactory outcome that the United States has not been able to bomb a single country within the former Warsaw

Pact and to this day has to play careful with Russia and her friends. This is because mutual assured destruction remains in effect: each side has enough nuclear weapons to obliterate the other. Since this is an affront to the American military ego, Americans have continued to preen and posture, announcing a defense doctrine that allows nuclear first strikes and actively pursuing the development of strategic missile defense. The Russians do not appear to be impressed. "We believe this strategic anti-missile defense system is somewhat chimerical, to put it mildly," said Sergei Ivanov, Russia's first deputy prime minister. "One can find a much cheaper response to any such system." The cheapest response I can think of is simply having Mr. Ivanov periodically stand up and say a few words.

Perhaps that is all the response the situation calls for, but Russia sells a lot of weapons, including a new generation of supersonic missiles and torpedoes, against which the US has no adequate defense, and successfully marketing them requires taking a stand in defense of national military prestige. And so we are bound to hear a great deal more about Americans destabilizing the security of Europe, and about Russia countering this threat with some anti-missile chimeras of their own — much cheaper ones. The United States needs a new Cold War to show itself and the world that it still matters, and Russia, finding the venture not too risky and quite profitable, is willing to hold up a mirror to American militarism. But the whole thing is a farce, and Vladimir Putin was quick to offer an old Russian saying by way of explaining it: "Don't blame the mirror if your face is crooked."

Russia has scaled back defense spending considerably since the Soviet collapse, but the defense budget of the United States has kept growing like a tumor and is on course to match and surpass what the entire rest of the world spends on defense. While one might naively assume that the rest of the world is quivering before such overwhelming military might, nothing of the sort is occurring. There is a little secret that everyone knows: the United States military does not know how to win. It just knows how to blow things up. Blowing things up may be fun, but it cannot be the only element in a winning strategy. The other key element is winning the peace once major combat operations are over, and here the mighty US military tends to fall squarely on its face and lay prone until political support for the war is withdrawn and the troops are brought back home. The United States could not conquer North Korea, resulting in the world's longest-running cease-fire. It is a stalemate punctuated by crises. The United States could not defeat the North Vietnamese with their underground tunnels and their primarily bicycle-based transportation system. The first Gulf War was precipitated by a misunderstanding caused by diplomatic incompetence: Saddam Hussein was a generally cooperative and helpful tyrant and all could have been resolved amicably had not April Glaspie, the US ambassador to Iraq, told him: "We have no opinion on your Arab-Arab conflicts, such as your dispute with Kuwait." Saddam took her at her word and thought that he could punish the Kuwaitis for stealing his oil. Bush Senior then proceeded to stand poor April on her head, declaring that "this will not stand!" The ensuing skirmish ended inconclusively, with Iraq humiliated and in stasis for a generation. This was considered a victory, with endless parades and much flag-waving. The US military was said to have recovered from "Vietnam syndrome." But nothing could hide the fact that it was a job left unfinished.

The more recent Iraq war is a full-blown, complete disaster, like Vietnam, or like Afghanistan was for the Soviets, but actually a lot worse, because Iraq is situated in the region which produces most of the oil. As a country, Iraq is effectively dead, and the longer US troops stay there, the worse the situation there becomes. The longer they wait to pull out, the worse it will be once they do. Iraq started out as a war of choice (a startlingly poor choice) but it is now a war of survival — certainly of America's status as a superpower, and quite possibly of its economic survival as well. Moreover, it is a war that appears to have already been lost. Sectarian and ethnic violence has been contained only because Americans have been paying the Iraqis not to fight each other, but will resume as soon as the Americans leave. In the summer of 2010, as the US pulls its last combat brigades out of Iraq, the Iraqis cannot even be bothered to form a government, knowing full well the scenario that is bound to unfold once the Americans finally leave.

The rest of America's recent military conflicts either consisted of or centered around a bombing campaign, and generally fall into one of two categories: strategic spoiling attacks, and attempts to bolster the presidential manhood. A strategic spoiling attack is a preventive action against a potential enemy who, if left unchecked, might attack you some time in the future. It is more or less a bullying tactic, and, as such, already an admission of defeat on the diplomatic front. One should prefer to live among strong friends, not weakened enemies.

Presidential manhood-bolstering bombing campaigns have come from both sides of the political spectrum (not much of a spectrum, it turns out, since both sides are shades of ultra-violent). There was the bombing of Panama, ostensibly to punish the apostate CIA asset Manuel Noriega, but really to mitigate against Bush Senior's so-called "wimp factor." There was also Clinton's despondent bombing of an aspirin factory in the Sudan and the bouncing around of some rocks in Afghanistan, ostensibly to punish terrorists for bombing US embassies in East Africa, but really to express frustration over the inordinate difficulties faced by the leader of the free world as a result of procuring oral sex. I feel his pain, but, to paraphrase Freud, sometimes a cruise missile isn't just a cruise missile.

It may appear that the US military is not capable of prevailing over any enemy, no matter how badly armed, demoralized or minuscule. While the Koreans and the Vietnamese were formidable, the US military could not bring to heel even the starving Somalis with their pickup trucks full of narcotic cud-chewing, Kalashnikov-toting youths. Nor could they pacify the Iraqis, even after softening them up with bombs and sanctions for more than a decade. There is one notable exception. If we look at any of the military conflicts that involved the US military since World War II, there is one that stands out as a complete success: the liberation of the tiny Caribbean island of Grenada. There, valiant American troops dislodged an unsavory and frightening Marxist regime which was supported by Cuba and Nicaragua and replaced it with a democratic, pro-American regime, much to the satisfaction of Grenada's Caribbean neighbors and cruising yachtsmen alike.

The Soviets never learned their lesson in Afghanistan. The slow, relentless, senseless carnage of that war did much to tarnish the image of the Red Army, which was until then still regarded as the people's champion for defeating Hitler and for standing up to the Americans. It took the disaster of the two campaigns in Chechnya after the Soviet collapse for the message to finally sink in. Russia eventually got Chechnya under control, through political rather than military means. A military effort alone can never defeat a popular insurgency. The insurgents never have to win, they just have to continue to fight. In fighting them, the military is forced to fight the people of the country, and by perpetuating a state of war it continually thwarts its stated purpose, which is to establish peace. There is no room for victory in this scenario, but only for an ever-widening spiral of murder, hatred and shame.

The lesson that the United States desperately needs to learn is that their trillion-dollar-a-year military is nothing more than a gigantic public money sponge that provokes outrage among friends and enemies alike and puts the country in ill repute. It is useless against its enemies, because they know better than to engage it directly. It can never be used to defeat any of the major nuclear powers, because sufficient deterrence against it can be maintained for relatively little money. It can never defuse a popular insurgency, because that takes political and diplomatic finesse, not a compulsion to bomb faraway places. Political and diplomatic finesse cannot be procured, even for a trillion dollars, even in a country that believes in extreme makeovers. As Vladimir Putin put it, "If grandmother had testicles, she'd be a grandfather."

The long sequence of American military failures in its many wars of choice may not be significant in and of itself. People throughout the world may cringe, but it is easy for Americans to consign these unhappy adventures to oblivion. They are skilled at rewriting, if not history, then at least their strangely foggy recollections of it. But at some point a key national interest becomes involved and the military adventure becomes more than just a way for the military to justify having an outsized budget. For the Soviets, this point came when they lost Afghanistan. They were in Afghanistan in accordance with the Brezhnev Doctrine, which stated unequivocally that no Socialist country would be allowed to backslide toward barbarous Capitalism. Once they let go of Afghanistan the tide turned, and the Communists had to let go of the Warsaw Pact, the Soviet Union, and finally Russia itself.

It is common knowledge that the US forces invaded Iraq for no adequately explained reason. What few people realize is that there is an American counterpart to the Brezhnev Doctrine. It is the Carter Doctrine, which states that the United States would use military force if necessary to defend its national interests in the Persian Gulf region. Carter announced it in a State of the Union speech in January of 1980, in response to the Soviet invasion of Afghanistan. It is in the national interest of the United States to be able to efficiently exploit the oil resources of Iraq and direct the resulting flow of oil to eager motorists back home. The military failure in Iraq (which as of this writing appears complete) is tantamount to a declaration that the Carter Doctrine is no longer in effect. The ensuing backslide will mean more than just the loss of Iraqi oil production; it may force the US out of the entire region. Coupled with other unhappy developments, such as the ongoing devaluation of the US dollar, widespread oil production shortfalls due to oil field depletion and increasing political instability in several oil-exporting countries, this may cause the US to lose access to oil in other regions as well. This will not make motorists back home happy. Moreover, it will spell the end of the American dream of global dominance and the definitive loss of superpower status.

After the Soviet Union collapsed, Russia faced a dilemma. It had stationed a great many troops abroad in Eastern Europe and particularly in East Germany. These troops were not all Russian: some were recruited from the various Soviet Republics, and their allegiance was to the Red Army — an entity that no longer existed. Repatriating and resettling these troops turned out to be a logistical nightmare. There was no housing and no jobs for the returning troops. But this was nothing compared to the problem that will be faced by the United States, which has over a thousand overseas military bases. The vast majority of these serve no vital purpose and are further examples of massive military bloat. In the coming years, starved of fuel and other resources, they will become worse than useless. Liquidating them and repatriating the troops will pose a far greater challenge than that faced by the Soviets. Amid the general confusion, some of the smaller military installations are likely to be simply forgotten, with the troops left to fend for themselves and their weapons going missing.

The last aspect of the superpower arms race worth mentioning is the arms sales race. The US and the SU both supplied weapons to their client states. The US conducted their arms trade on better terms, by lending the client state money with which to buy the weapons or by forcing the client state to spend its oil export revenue on weapons systems. The Soviets more or less gave their weapons away to the brotherly peoples they held in their sway. Russia, which inherited most of the Soviet defense industry, has updated its business plan, and is now positioned to surpass the United States in weapons sales. Military defeats do not make for successful weapons marketing campaigns.

World's Jailers

The jails race once showed the Soviets with a decisive lead, thanks to their innovative Gulag program. Under Lenin, and later under Stalin, millions of people were herded into labor camps to provide slave labor for massive construction projects such as the Belomor Canal, which links the Baltic to the North Sea. Over the years, the inmate population was comprised not only of criminals, who were always plentiful, but also of aristocrats associated with the ancien régime who were not fleet enough to emigrate to a new career of driving taxicabs in Berlin, Paris or New York. The inmates also included ethnic minorities such as the Chechens (who found themselves in disfavor after they welcomed the Nazi invaders), soldiers who had surrendered to the enemy instead of dying heroically (surrender was considered a form of desertion), priests and nuns (to rid the country of unscientific "religious superstitions") and plenty of innocent bystanders, who were swept up by a well-oiled judiciary machine. The arrests often happened in the middle of the night and those arrested simply vanished from society. Their disappearance was studiously ignored and the families of the disappeared were shunned by society. Society was afraid, but since any admission of fear could be misinterpreted as an admission of guilt (of suspecting that the system itself was criminal), even the fear had to remain hidden.

After Stalin's death, a gradual liberalization took place. Many of those falsely accused and imprisoned were rehabilitated, often posthumously. Thereafter, the ranks of the political prisoners shrank steadily. The appearance of Alexander Solzhenitsyn's *The Gulag Archipelago* became a watershed event, lifting the veil on a secret parallel universe, with its own language and customs, yet one that was very recognizably Soviet. It could operate in the shadows, but once thrust into the broad light of day it immediately became obvious for what it was: a world-class abomination, on par with the Nazi holocaust.

A popular movement developed, devoted to keeping track of prisoners of conscience and communicating their names to foreign news sources. The resulting external pressure on the Soviet government made it difficult for the judiciary meat grinder to operate normally. The monsters running this system generally did not crave parading their monstrousness before a world audience, and this gradually starved the system of new blood. Near the end, under General Secretary Andropov, there was an attempt to stem the tide by rounding up a few dissidents, who by this time had grown quite bold in their opposition, but it was futile and died along with Andropov when he, as it were, dropped off. And so the Soviet Union gradually fell behind in the jails race. By the time the Soviet Union fell apart, its worst atrocities had started to recede into history. There were no widespread calls for reprisals against those who had committed them, who were by then either retired or dead.

In the end the jails race has been won by the Americans, who are currently holding the world record for the percentage of population held in jail. Here, the judiciary meat grinder relies less on secrecy than on obscurity, gorging itself on the poor and the defenseless, while being careful around the moneyed and the privileged. To mask its naked aggression against its citizens, the United States has traditionally used the fig leafs of constitutional rights and due process. But the ill winds now blowing across the country have wilted this decorative flora, and not a week seems to go by without some new reports of abuses or atrocities.

The American justice system favors the educated, the corporations and the rich, and takes unfair advantage of the uneducated, the private citizen and the poor. It would seem that almost any legal entanglement can be resolved through the judicious application of money, while almost any tussle with the law can result in financial penalties and even imprisonment for those who are forced to rely on public defenders. In essence, any sufficiently complex system of laws is inherently unjust, favoring those few who have the resources to grapple with its extreme complexity. This is clearly the case in the United States where, in civil disputes, those with more money can almost always prevail over those with less, simply by threatening to sue.

Many people believe that a criminal is someone who commits a criminal act. This is not true, at least not in the American system of justice. Here, a criminal is someone who has been accused of committing a criminal act, tried for it and found guilty. Whether or not that person has in fact committed the act is immaterial: witnesses may lie, evidence can be fabricated, juries can be manipulated. On the other hand, a person who has committed a criminal act but has not been tried for it, or has been tried and exonerated, is not a criminal, and for anyone to call him a criminal is libelous.

It therefore follows that, within the American justice system, committing a crime and getting away with it is substantially identical to not committing a crime at all. Wealthy clients have lawyers who are constantly testing and, whenever possible, expanding the bounds of legality. Corporations have entire armies of lawyers and can almost always win against individuals. Furthermore, corporations use their political influence to promote the use of binding arbitration, which favors them, as the way to resolve disputes.

The US is by no means unique in jailing or executing innocents and in neglecting to punish the guilty. But while in other countries such injustices can be put down to corruption, oppression or other problems with the justice system, in the US they are designed into the justice system itself. This state of affairs makes it hopelessly naive for anyone to confuse legality with morality, ethics or justice.

You should always behave in a legal manner, but this will not necessarily save you from going to jail. In what manner you choose to behave legally is between you and your conscience, God or lawyer, if you happen to have one, and may or may not have anything to do with obeying laws. Legality is a property of the justice system, while justice is an ancient virtue. This distinction is lost on very few people: most people possess a sense of justice and, separate from it, an understanding of what is legal and what they can get away with.

The US legal system, as it stands, offers a fine luxury model, but its budget model is manifestly unsafe. It is good for those who can afford it and bad for those who cannot. In recent years, appalling numbers of those awaiting execution have been exonerated as a result of DNA testing. This amounts to an attempted murder rate high enough to condemn the entire criminal justice system that is responsible for it and, at the very least, ban everyone involved in it from further public service. But nothing of the sort is likely to happen, since most of the victims are poor and are therefore of no consequence to the larger system.

As ever-increasing numbers of people find themselves lapsing into poverty, they will also find that they cannot pay what it takes to secure a good legal outcome for themselves. They will start to see the system not as one of justice but as a tool of oppression, and will learn to avoid it rather than look to it for help. As oppression becomes the norm, at some point the pretense to be serving justice will be dispensed with in favor of a much simpler, efficient, streamlined system of social control, perhaps one based on martial law. To some extent, this shift has already occurred. America now has secret jails, indefinite detention, secret tribunals, Soviet-style show trials, torture of prisoners, family detention for those who happen to cross US-controlled territory without the proper papers and psychiatric imprisonment for both adults and children, where they are subjected to regimens of experimental anti-psychotic drugs.

Those who bemoan the out-of-control American criminal justice system would like to find ways to make it more effective. But perhaps the real problem is that it is too effective, and needs to become much less so. It is obvious that the jails race serves the purposes of the law enforcement class, providing them with employment, status and ample funds. But it bears pointing out that it serves the interests of the criminal class even better. The prison system offers many services to criminals: it allows them to congregate, network and hold seminars on the finer points of criminal technique and new ways to commit bigger and better crimes without getting caught. Furthermore, it gives criminals a periodic sabbatical, making room for two million more criminals than the victim population could otherwise sustain, ensuring that whenever there arises a fruitful opportunity to commit a crime, an ample supply of well-rested and highly trained specialists is available to make use of it.

The rationale for imprisoning over two million people in the United States — the world's highest rate of incarceration — is that it deters crime. Sociologists slice and dice crime statistics looking for a correlation between increased rates of incarceration and decreased crime rates. The best they seem to be able to find is a correlation of about 0.25 between an increased rate of incarceration and a decrease in the crime rate. That is, the measurable effect of incarceration levels on crime levels is not significant enough to state that an increase in the former causes a decrease in the latter. More evidence would be needed to declare that the mass incarceration program is in any sense functional. It is sometimes possible to find a stronger correlation between, say, rain dances and rainfall amounts.

While the criminal justice system seems like an effective way to promote crime, it may be even more effective in serving the atavistic desire of the population to see punishment doled out, which in more barbaric times brought crowds to gaze up at the sacrificial altar atop a pyramid, or the scaffold, the stake or the guillotine, and which even today brings a strange glint to the eyes of American elected leaders when the subject of capital punishment comes up during political debates. It is in the nature of powerless people to vicariously enjoy the exercise of arbitrary power by others.

Whereas the Nazis had to tattoo identification numbers on their concentration camp victims, Americans now have access to more modern technology, such as implantable radio-frequency identification (RFID) tags, biometric and face-recognition systems, satellite surveillance, ubiquitous surveillance cameras and globally networked databases. These can theoretically enable the United States to turn much of the planet into a single large Gulag, or at least to overextend itself and collapse while trying. This trend is currently being exemplified by the State of California, which by itself has the third largest incarceration system in the world. It is going bankrupt, forcing it to parole tens of thousands of inmates. This strategy is encountering diminishing returns, because the recidivism rate is 70 percent, making California law enforcement akin to sport fishing, but in reverse: instead of "catch and release," it keeps the fish in a fish tank and, for something to do, practices "release and catch." In spite of massive prison overcrowding, the inmates keep coming back for more: life on the inside may be a bit confining but it is generally carefree, while life on the outside may be exciting for a time but is fraught with difficulties and temptations, and so the inmates struggle to find a life-jail balance.

When the American system of mass incarceration finally collapses, its surviving victims, who have no experience of anything better, will likely perpetuate this culture of abuse at an ever lower and more miserable level. At this point, there is really very little to be done about the American culture of crime — except suffer from it, reaping what has already been sown. The long-term effect of perpetuating an unequal and unjust social order, amplified by a program of mass imprisonment, is to create a vast society of victims.

Evil Empires

When Ronald Reagan referred to the Soviet Union as the "evil empire," this label, impolitic though it was, made sense to a great number of people and the label stuck. But what a difference two decades can make! Shortly after Reagan stood at the Brandenburg Gate in Berlin and spoke the words, "Mr. Gorbachev, tear down this wall!" the Berlin Wall was indeed broken down into souvenir-sized pieces, but twenty years later big political walls are again fashionable, except now it is Americans and their clients that are putting them up. There is a wall along the US–Mexican border, countless walls carving up Palestine into a pattern Jimmy Carter accurately labeled as "apartheid," a currently stalled plan to partition Baghdad into Shiite and Sunni ghettos and numerous walls within the US itself around gated communities and exclusive compounds.

For an American, hiding behind a wall is becoming an increasingly good idea. Over the last two decades, memory of the Soviet Union has faded from view, while the United States has taken its place as the symbol of all that is evil throughout much of Europe, the Muslim countries and many other parts of the world. Wherever there is public protest — be it against war, injustice, globalization, violations of human rights, environmental destruction or policies that accelerate catastrophic climate change — it is the United States that offers a conveniently large and easy target. While much of the population throughout the world is dead set against cooperation with the United States, their political leaders have to be careful: the United States is still a little too powerful to oppose directly. On the other hand, any appearance of overt appeasement of American ambitions has come to spell automatic disaster at the polls, so the politicians stall and bide their time.

As the ultimately futile nine-year Soviet occupation of Afghanistan wore on, the economy stagnated and a succession of dour, gray-faced, geriatric General Secretaries succeeded each other atop the Lenin mausoleum, a number of people within the higher echelons of the Communist party started to find their evilness somewhat humiliating. The imperial status was non-negotiable, as was the socialist ideology, but some sort of workaround strategy was clearly required for the evilness bit. Gorbachev gave voice to these official yearnings through his glasnost and perestroika campaigns. A great number of partial excuses, of the "mistakes were made" variety, were offered.

I remember a certain conversation that took place around that time, in the late '80s. The topic of discussion was, "What could these bastards (meaning the Soviet government) possibly want now? "A wizened old lady offered an answer that seemed nonsensical at first, but made a lot of sense upon reflection: they want shame. They are tired of being bad as in "evil"; now they just want to be bad as in "not very good." They are even willing to feel a little bit ashamed about it and to offer some vaguely worded apologies, provided that these fall well short of them actually accepting any responsibility. You see, evil and incompetence do not mix. Our imagination cannot conceive of the Devil who would have your immortal soul in a jiffy, if only he could locate the paperwork. It's one Hell of a mess down there. The demons who handle the paperwork have become so lazy it's a sin. "To hell with them!" the Devil would like to say, but that's where they reside already, plus he can't recall the details of who lost what when, and so there is nothing to be done. As mistakes continue to be made, the sinners can breathe more easily.

Twenty years later, it is the American officials that are making a spectacular show of their incompetence. But rather than mincing words Gorbachev-style, the Americans are able to achieve a wonderful theatrical effect, thanks to their plain-spoken, straight-talking President. From "Mission accomplished," spoken as the Iraqi insurgency takes off, to "Brownie, you're doing a heck of a job!" as New Orleans drowns, to many other, similarly preposterous statements, we hear a Presidential clarion call to national incompetence. It is a mistake to view such utterances as gaffes or blunders or flights of whimsy: they are true thought leadership. Other high officials have their own strategies: the Vice President pretends to be delusional, producing a steady stream of strongly worded statements of fiction, while the former Attorney General simulates early onset Alzheimer's with a compelling display of fogged memory. Other administration officials make a show of accidentally destroying important documents but, for added effect, they destroy them incompetently, so that copies are soon retrieved. American officials at all levels should fall in line with this brilliant strategy that has been handed down to them from on high as stone tablets from Mount Sinai. Should they fail to do so, history will remember them as evil. Should they succeed, history will mercifully consign their memory to oblivion, judging them to be merely incompetent.

Bankruptcy

For several decades now, the US dollar has been able to keep its value in the face of ever larger trade and fiscal imbalances largely because it has been the world's reserve currency and the currency most of the world used when buying oil. Other nations have been forced to export products to the United States because this is the only way for them to gather the dollars they need to purchase oil. This has produced a continuous windfall for the US Treasury. This state of affairs is coming to an end: as more and more oil-producing nations find alternative ways of doing business with their customers, trading oil for Euros or food, the US dollar erodes in value. As the dollar drops in value, the price of an ever-increasing list of essential imports goes up, driving up inflation. At some point, inflation will start to feed on itself and will give rise to hyperinflation.

If your immediate thought is, "Hyperinflation in the US? Impossible!" then you are certainly not alone. A lot of regular people have trouble thinking about the possibility of hyperinflation, not just the economists. Hyperinflation, they say, requires the government to emit vast amounts of money, which, being a good, prudent government, it simply will not do. But this government is drowning in red ink and will do what desperate governments have always done: opt for inflating its debt away rather than defaulting on it, to retain at least some spending ability in the face of a collapsing tax base and dried-up foreign credit. The people at the Fed do have to be kept fed, after all.

Some of those who doubt the inevitability of hyperinflation point to the weakness of trade unions, and say that workers in the US are too poorly organized to bargain collectively and secure cost of living adjustments that would propel the economy along an inflationary spiral. These people seem to feel that the workers will somehow continue to be able to work even as their entire paycheck disappears as they buy gasoline for their daily commute. They remind me of the proverbial farmer who trained his horse to stop eating and almost succeeded, but unfortunately the horse died first. Those who have work that needs to be done will have to make it physically possible for someone to do it.

There are also plenty of people in the US — the ones who are closer to the top of the economic food chain or just feel like they are — who will pay themselves whatever they require, giving themselves, and those upon whose loyalty they must depend, any cost of living adjustment they deem necessary. They will continue doing so until they are bankrupt. Because wealth is distributed so unevenly, these people make a disproportionately large difference.

Perhaps the difficulty in reconciling oneself to the possibility of a worthless US dollar stems from history and culture, not economics. Unlike the Russians or the Germans, whose historical memory includes one or more episodes of hyperinflation, it is hard for Americans to imagine living in a time when their paper money is not worth its weight in toilet paper. But such conditions have been known to occur. Savings boil off into the ether. People who still receive paychecks or retirement checks cash them immediately, and do their best to buy the things they need to survive as quickly as they can, before the prices go up again.

Coming to terms with the possibility of hyperinflation is a bit of a challenge for many Americans. They even have serious problems discussing ordinary garden-variety inflation. The common experience of inflation is almost entirely unrelated to the way it is understood by America's economists. When the costs of housing, education and health care continuously go up by double-digit percentages annually, you and I might think of that as inflation: everything costs us more. But the economists would beg to differ: these price increases are not inflationary. When house prices go up, you and I might think that there is housing inflation, but the economists would contend that it's asset appreciation, which is good for you. But when the housing market collapses a few years later, forcing the federal government to step in as a guarantor of last resort for trillions in underwater mortgages and fraudulent collateralized debt obligations, economists spin around on their heels, snap their fingers, and start talking about deflation, which is bad.

With the vast majority of America's mainstream economists apparently living on cloud-cuckoo-land and speaking in nursery rhymes, inflation, to most people, remains a bit of a mystery. All of our problems can be made to sound almost arbitrarily complicated. Perhaps, if you are an economist, there is simply no money in keeping things simple. And so economists have many different classifications of money/debt, some sitting quietly, others circulating sluggishly. With the entire US economy now a bad credit risk, generating new debt has become problematic, and as existing debt is written off or paid down, the overall amount of money in the economy decreases, as does spending, depressing demand and forcing prices lower, thereby causing deflation as far as the eye can see. Still, can't the government just print and hand out so much money as to cause hyperinflation anyway? Of course it can! But even if the government decides to turn off the printing presses and just let everyone starve while watching the economy crumble, we can be sure hyperinflation will eventually occur in any case.

The extent to which we value money depends on our degree of confidence in the economy. At first, as the economy starts to collapse, we start to hoard money, to make sure that we don't run out. Then, as the economy continues to wither away, supply disruptions and price spikes cause some of us to suddenly realize that we might not be able to gain access to the things we need for much longer, never mind the cost, and that running out of money is not fatal whereas running out of food, fuel and other supplies certainly can be. And then we start cashing in our paper assets in exchange for physical commodities we think might be more useful. Shortly thereafter everyone realizes that the chips they are holding are not all that valuable any more. It is this realization, more than anything else, that renders the chips instantly worthless. There is little doubt that economists will use the term "volatility" to describe what is happening, and assure us that growth will resume once it has run its course. For a time, hyperinflation in commodities may be accompanied by even faster deflation in suburban real estate and other types of stranded assets, wiping out the collateral value of whatever debt instruments still remain intact. After that, the government will face a choice: print money and spend it, or close up shop. When confronted with this choice, governments have usually been observed to print money.

Beyond the mere indignity of having to rush around with bundles of worthless paper, national bankruptcy brings more serious effects. One is that a large segment of the population — pensioners and others on fixed incomes — are left penniless. Another is that imports grow scarce. In the case of the United States, which imports two-thirds of its oil and a large proportion of its consumer goods, this will mean gasoline shortages, blackouts and empty shelves in stores. These are accompanied by a credit crunch, which makes it impossible to finance new projects. The combined effect of these disruptions causes business activity to slow to a crawl and personal incomes to plummet, driving down government revenues, in turn causing government services to be curtailed.

For most people in the US, rich or poor, life without money is unthinkable. They may want to give this problem some thought, ahead of time.

Collapse of Legitimacy

For each of the two superpowers, their sense of identity has been firmly rooted in their singular ideology — either socialism or capitalism. It is their extreme adherence to one or the other that has doomed their societies, and economies, in the long run. All of the more successful developed nations are both socialist and capitalist to different degrees, because by this point in time it is very well understood that ideology has its limits. The profit motive has to be tempered somehow to serve the needs of society at large if that society as a whole, and not just the minority that controls the capital, is to succeed. Likewise, relinquishing all control of the economy to ponderous government bureaucracies is unlikely to produce a rosy economic scenario. In the healthier democracies, a broad political spectrum stands in the way of profiteering within the public sector in areas such as education or medicine, as well as thwarting attempts to over-regulate industry.

Thus, the purely capitalist or the purely socialist country is like a stroke patient who denies the existence of her right or left hand. The fact that the ideological distinction is artificial was first spotted by Albert Camus, who pointed out that both Western industrialism and its communist version achieve similar results through similar means — industrialization and specialization of labor. In the 1950s, in *Défense de L'Homme Révolté*, Camus accurately predicted that if the communist experiment were to fail, this would be misunderstood as an ideological victory by the West.

Camus also indicated a specific failure of both systems: their inability to provide creative, meaningful work. We see this failure in the very high rates of depression. We attempt to define depression as a psychological ailment, but it is a symptom of a cultural failure: the inability to make life meaningful or enjoyable. Depression in the face of depressing circumstances is a symptom of unconscious rebellion. Although the rebellious can be and often are medicated into submission, this does not address the underlying problem.

To be fair, the United States is far more socialist than the Soviet Union was capitalist. The dead hand of Soviet central planners put a curse on just about every type of entrepreneurial endeavor, from agriculture to fashion accessories. Exceptions were made for certain national champions — technological concerns that produced weapons or aircraft or other technology products. Cultural activities were less victimized by central planning than by ideological control, but in areas where ideology and planning did not matter the country did quite well.

The United States features many aspects of socialism — many more than it is willing to admit to. For instance, there is a great deal of empty talk about private retirement, but it turns out that most retirees are critically dependent on Social Security, and would starve without it. Likewise, Medicare provides the services needed to keep the elderly alive longer; without it, life expectancy would plummet, just like it did in Russia after the gradual disappearance of socialized medicine following the Soviet collapse. The government also pays for most of the transportation infrastructure (neglecting railroads, for historical reasons), and heavily subsidizes industrial agriculture. No modern industrial economy can survive without direct government investment in industry and the United States is no exception. Because of ideological constraints, the United States government cannot do this openly and effectively; it must instead support its industrial base via the ever-expanding defense budget. This is very inefficient, since the products in which this investment results are largely useless and, when used, destroy wealth rather than create it.

In the United States, there is also a fair amount of melding between government and private structures, especially in the area of medicine. Since the melding cannot be overt, it is effected by means of an institutional device known as the "revolving door," which allows specialists to circulate between the private and the public sector, taking their projects with them. Thus it turns out that, over time, those who regulate new drugs also work for the companies that profit from them. This scheme is far more susceptible to corruption than outright government management of business, but far more conducive to extracting a profit, both from government budgets and from the population.

Having an ideology is all well and good, but it actually has to work in terms of providing a satisfactory life for much of the population. The Soviet model failed when it became obvious that it simply was not keeping up: the average worker in a Western nation fared much better than the average worker in the worker's paradise that communism was committed to producing. The American model of supposedly unadulterated capitalism is producing steadily sinking fortunes for the vast majority, but is propped up by the fact that it allows a small minority to become fabulously rich, coupled with the notion that you (or any random person) could somehow miraculously become one of them. There is also a pathological fiction known as the "American Dream," which is aggressively promoted by the media and finds most of its victims among the working class. It consists of the notion that diligent work and playing by the rules will make you successful. Masquerading as hope, it gains its effectiveness from a perversion of pride, a psychological trick people choose to play on themselves to obscure their powerlessness. They can sense that they are oppressed, and they can see that rebelling against this oppression would be futile, and so their last prideful stand is to pretend that their failures are of their own making, even if they have been most conveniently arranged for them by their oppressors.

Both the Soviet Union and the United States devoted a great deal of fanfare to publicizing their democratic institutions — much more than these institutions deserved. Far more democratic countries make far less noise about their democratic institutions — they simply take them for granted because they work. The Soviet electoral system was one of coerced consent: the Communist party selected candidates and the voters were compelled to either vote for them, by depositing an unmarked ballot in an urn, or to vote against them, by crossing out the ballot under the watchful eyes of election officials. Needless to say, most candidates sailed into office with astronomically high poll numbers. The American electoral system is one of optional false choice: the one uniquely meaningful choice that is perennially missing is "none of the above."

The Soviet Union had a single, entrenched, systemically corrupt political party, which held a monopoly on power. The US has two entrenched, systemically corrupt political parties, whose positions are often indistinguishable and which together hold a monopoly on power. In either case, there is, or was, a single governing elite, but in the United States it organizes itself into opposing teams to make its stranglehold on power seem more sportsmanlike. It is certainly more sporting to have two capitalist parties go at each other than just having the one communist party to vote for. The things they fight over in public are generally symbolic little tokens of social policy, chosen for ease of public posturing. The Communist party offered just one bitter pill. The two capitalist parties offer a choice of two placebos. The latest innovation is the photo finish election, where each party pre-purchases exactly 50 percent of the vote through largely symmetrical allocation of campaign resources and the result is pulled out of statistical noise, like a rabbit out of a hat. It is a tribute to the intelligence of the American people that so few of them bother to vote.

Both the Soviet Union and the United States were very aggressive in spreading their ideologies and systems of government around the world. The Soviet Union expanded its sphere of influence over Eastern Europe as a side effect of repelling German aggression. In other parts of the world, it looked for openings, providing support wherever people revolted against colonial regimes and Western exploitation. It was a poor bargain for their clients, entered into out of ignorance or desperation, that traded economic exploitation for political oppression. The United States generally could not draw on public support in expanding its sphere of influence and relied on various other techniques, such as political assassinations (as in Iran, Iraq and Chile), which were often carried out through proxies. Outright invasion was tried on a few occasions, with very mixed success. But another technique, which went under the guise of promoting economic development, worked quite well for a time. Here, a country's natural resources were developed and exploited by providing development assistance. The proceeds of such development were usually expatriated and deposited in Western banks rather than reinvested within the country. The assistance took the form of loans, which were partly embezzled by the country's pro-Western elites, with the remainder used to pay American companies to develop the resources. The country itself was saddled with the costs of debt repayment. The loans were usually overly generous, making the job lucrative for American companies, while also making sure that the country would remain in debt forever. If it became unable to service its debt, the International Monetary Fund came in and imposed austerity conditions. Countries that managed to escape the stranglehold of the IMF and the World Bank generally did better than those that didn't.

In recent years, the United States has also attempted to stage-manage democratic revolutions in various unfortunate countries that were formerly part of the Soviet sphere of influence. These were the work of the Color Revolution Syndicate. They were well-organized, foreign-financed events that involved mass production and shipping in of flags and t-shirts, promotion via international mass media, coordinated political pressure from Western governments and even catering services for the demonstrators, who were mostly young, bored and did not need much of an excuse to go and demonstrate. They demonstrated for freedom and democracy and while the freedom in question was mainly intended for foreign corporations and democracy was to stand for money politics and stage-managed elections, such subtleties were lost on their simple minds. The trial run was conducted in Serbia in 2000. The Rose Revolution in long-suffering Georgia was likewise a success, and involved switching an old pro-Western stooge, Shevardnadze, for a younger one, Saakashvili, to secure Georgia's role as a US-dominated "Pipelineistan." But there the success streak ended. The Orange Revolution in the Ukraine ended in the travesty of a permanently dysfunctional government. The Tulip Revolution in Kyrgyzstan resulted in a new government that was not only horribly corrupt and quite friendly toward Moscow, but that was also later overthrown in a bloody populist uprising. The Cedar Revolution in Lebanon resulted in a Hezbollah takeover and an ensuing Israeli invasion. The halfheartedly attempted non-colored revolution in Belarus ended in a yawn and a whimper.

The Color Revolution Syndicate seems spent for now, having achieved very little, but there is a new effort to generate media noise for internal consumption, to perpetuate the fiction that something, somewhere, is going America's way. As an example, take the Western, and particularly American, press coverage devoted to the April 2007 anti-government demonstrations in Moscow and St. Petersburg, with the former chess master Gary Kasparov as a cheerleader. Nobody in the Western press bothered to mention that Kasparov is connected with the US neoconservative movement, or that the demonstrators were a ragtag assemblage of nationalists, die-hard *perestroika* Communists and students, many of whom were paid to show up. Any Russian with the slightest bit of political sense can tell that Kasparov does not have Russia's best interests in mind. But this is irrelevant: his gambit is strictly for foreign consumption.

This, and other similarly delusional efforts to rekindle the Cold War, signal the desperation felt by the American propagandists. With the effort to invade Iraq and Afghanistan a resounding defeat, with the wider War on Terror only succeeding in doubling the number of terrorist attacks, and with a war against Iran unwinnable even as a board game played by retired generals, the US desperately needs an enemy to justify having a military that cannot win. This enemy must be safe to rail against, but obviously too powerful to attack directly, leaving a proud and purposeful paralysis as the only possible choice of action. The fact that Russia remains largely indifferent to these hostile overtures makes this an innocuous but humiliating farce. If, to use President Bush's expression, "We're not winning; we're not losing," then we would at least hope to be exceptionally annoying. But what if our supposed enemies cannot even be provoked to the point of annoyance? Wherefore then, O mighty superpower?

The Collapse Gap

IN CHAPTER 2, I showed how the two superpowers, the extant United States and the defunct Soviet Union, were not too dissimilar to disallow a fruitful comparison of the two. The elements that caused the latter to collapse, economically and politically, appear quite likely to bring down the former at some unspecified time (estimates vary). There are those who would take this to mean that both superpowers are richly deserving of ignominy for the viciousness of their methods, of ridicule for their fruitlessness and of disdain for the hypocrisy of the ideologies they respectively proffered in defense of these methods. Those who wish to feast at this banquet of negative emotion might find that the USSR no longer looks appetizing, while the USA is still very much on the menu. We, however, have something more important to discuss: Where is your meal ticket really going to come from? Are you still hoping that it will be issued by a superpower? If so, what is your back-up plan?

A superpower (whichever one you happen to prefer) in some ways resembles a normal country, in that it provides all the essential life-support services to the people who inhabit its domain. Like a supernova that briefly outshines all other stars, a superpower's social services can be quite lavish, for a time. Whether directly or indirectly, it can provide food and shelter, medical care, the means for getting around, education for one's children, support in old age and so on. If any of these is withdrawn (as can happen swiftly, as our figurative supernova collapses into a black hole or a neutron star), a great many people are adversely affected; some of them even die. It is therefore important to focus on these key services, and see how they fare in an economic collapse and the upheaval and paralysis that follow it. While the Soviet Union provided most of these key services using the public sector, the population of the United States is critically dependent on the private sector for most, if not all, of them. We will find that this arrangement may provide a higher standard of living while the economy is still functioning, but is far from optimal for survival once it shuts down.

Collapses in General

In Chapter 1, I described what I observed when the Soviet Union collapsed. I don't see why what happens to the United States should be entirely dissimilar, at least in general terms. The specifics are different and we will get to them in a moment. We should certainly expect shortages of fuel, food, medicine and countless consumer items, outages of electricity, gas and water, breakdowns in transportation systems and other infrastructure, hyperinflation, widespread shutdowns and mass layoffs, along with a lot of despair, confusion, violence and lawlessness. We definitely should not expect any grand rescue plans, innovative technology programs, or miracles of social cohesion.

We should expect the political establishment to remain intact, at least initially, and to attempt to keep up appearances, while suffering progressive paralysis due to its inability to spend money in the manner to which it has become accustomed. The signal event that brought the Soviet experiment to a close was the inability of the government to expand and roll over its foreign debt. The United States is now approaching a similar point of no return with regard to its level of indebtedness. Whereas the Soviets had to export energy in order to import food, the US has to import energy with which to produce and distribute food. In either case, the sudden inability to continue going deeper into debt is what triggers the final economic convulsion.

Once the financial equation no longer has a solution, the government becomes crippled. Authorities at every level will no longer command respect. Law enforcement will be overwhelmed, replaced in part by private security and hastily organized local self-defense units. Many laws will be universally ignored. We should also expect the maintenance of every type of infrastructure, both public and private, from roads and bridges to water and sewage, from public utilities to transportation systems, to be either rationed or foregone altogether, causing many disasters, large and small. Municipal services, such as garbage removal, will be either curtailed or halted entirely. Fuel deliveries to remote locations will no longer occur, and places that are not survivable without central heating or air conditioning will become uninhabitable, producing a flood of internal refugees.

We should definitely not expect any grand new mitigation projects, because under such conditions no long-term planning is possible. The horizon for planning activities will be the same week, if not the same day, and large new projects will not even be considered. The mind-bending difficulties of securing funding in a hyperinflationary era, of procuring supplies in a time of shortages and widespread looting and hoarding, and assorted logistical nightmares caused by the breakdown of the transportation system, will make any attempted big new projects more likely to turn out like the recent Iraqi reconstruction project than like the Marshall Plan. Thus, all successful adaptations to the new circumstances will have to be made at the local level, and will have to rely on existing infrastructure, inventory and locally available talents and skills.

When faced with such developments, some people are quick to realize what they have to do to survive and start doing these things, generally without permission. A new sort of economy emerges, completely informal, and often semi-criminal. It revolves around liquidating and recycling the remains of the old economy. It is based on direct access to resources and the threat of force, rather than ownership or legal authority. People who have a problem with this way of doing business quickly find themselves out of the game, but the time of transition is fraught with danger, especially for those who remain in denial.

A particular danger is posed by those who wish to restore law and order and refuse to acknowledge the fact that the old rules no longer apply. The combination of a burgeoning black market and continuing attempts at law enforcement raises the stakes for even relatively innocuous activities, such as selling contraband tobacco, giving rise to an unnecessarily high level of violence. Since black-market entrepreneurs are usually better armed and more highly incentivized than the defenders of the status quo, there tends to be a high attrition rate among the latter, and the more intelligent of them start to seek accommodation with the former. This can hardly be characterized as corruption, which is a distortion of an extant system; rather, it should properly be regarded as a process of political and cultural transformation. During the least settled post-Soviet years in the mid–1990s, certain Russian officials could be accurately described as "members of government/mafia." Bribery became perfectly acceptable and expected; the level of government services one received depended on the level of one's gratitude for receiving them, expressed in financial terms. For many Russian entrepreneurs official extortion came to be seen as simply another cost of doing business, while those who were still angered by the new system could more properly be characterized as simply mad.

The beginnings of this process can already be seen in the more disrupted parts of the United States, such as Louisiana, which has failed to recover from the social damage of Hurricane Katrina, and Arizona, which, along with many other states, is being invaded by the Mexican narcomafia in the wake of the lost "war on drugs." The criminal class, flush with cash and armed with AK–47s (the weapon of choice of armed insurgents the world over), is being ineffectually opposed by increasingly underfunded and under-equipped police armed with handguns. We should expect that, once this process has run its course, Mexican narco-barons will become Arizona's new aristocracy, supplanting the likes of Senator John McCain.

With the official economy at a standstill, the old capital, consisting of stocks, bonds and cash, quickly becomes worthless. Almost without exception, these bits of paper derive their value from the promise of uninterrupted economic activity and growth. Much of the capital equipment used for transportation, such as car, truck and airplane fleets, becomes inoperable and unmaintainable without cheap and plentiful fuel (diesel, gasoline and jet fuel), without which they become stranded assets, worth their weight in scrap metal. In turn, as money flees stocks and bonds, commodity prices are bid up, the price of scrap skyrockets, and these stranded assets are rapidly dismantled, crushed or melted down, and exported to the remaining industrialized nations. The few bits of valuable scientific and industrial equipment are carefully crated up and exported, along with art objects and antiques. In an environment where most business activity revolves around cannibalizing what remains of the old economy, personal connections, favors and physical access to needed supplies are the only stores of value on which one can continue to rely.

With the nominal, official government powerless to control the situation, or even to influence the course of events, new power structures arise. Elements of organized crime, urban gangs, former military, military contractors and freelancers and former law enforcement, amalgamate to various extents, in what is sure to be a very messy and bloody process. Where these elements become separated by racial or ethnic divides, civil conflicts may erupt, which, if left unchecked, may descend into ethnic cleansing and genocide. While the former Soviet Union's largest trouble spot was Chechnya, the United States is riddled with areas where ethnic and racial divides sometimes erupt into armed conflict. For instance, Los Angeles is a scene of a continuous low-level civil war between black and Latino gangs. Once they are no longer harried by the LAPD or the narcs they may be able to sort themselves out, but an equally likely eventual outcome is a rather less populous, racially cleansed Los Angeles where, outside of a few well-defended enclaves, English is spoken at the risk of catching a bullet.

In many places, provided one's life is not immediately threatened by lack of food, water or shelter, or by violence, life simply slows to a crawl. The rush hour traffic is gone and multi-lane highways that were previously packed with cars are reclaimed for other, improvised uses, such as trailer parks, open air markets and shantytowns. On a previously busy thoroughfare, a single school bus might roll through two or three times a day, slowly picking its way between potholes on the one open lane, transporting adults rather than children, with the rest of the traffic made up of a steady trickle of bicycles and pedestrians. For most people, the world at large will once again become relegated to the realm of storytelling and fiction, while the real world shrinks down to the patch of ground they can cover on foot and the people they encounter along the way.

These are the generalities. Now let's look at some specifics.

Energy

Nowhere is the difference between the two superpowers more glaring, and more significant for their relative chances of making a comeback in the wake of collapse, than in the area of energy production. For both the United States and the Soviet Union, their ability to dominate the planet for a time was based on their military might, which was made possible by their vast industrial base, which in turn required massive inputs of raw materials and energy. Ultimately, their superpower status was predicated on the availability of cheap and plentiful crude oil — so cheap that its price never became a limiting factor for growth, and so plentiful that its supply could increase decade after decade.

The Soviet Union did not need to import energy, and to this day Russia remains one of the world's largest oil producers and exporters. The production and distribution system faltered, but never collapsed. Price controls kept the lights on even as hyperinflation raged. There were some supply disruptions, some of which froze out certain remote settlements, especially in the Arctic. But the energy supply system proved to be much more resilient than the political system or the economy overall. It was designed as an almost purely physical system, decoupled from any mental elements of market psychology: material was dug up or pumped, processed, shipped and consumed, according to an allocation scheme, under central control. And yet there is every reason to think that the Soviet Union succumbed to Peak Oil. Soviet oil production reached its all-time peak around 1988, and just three years later the country was bankrupt and, shortly thereafter, dissolved politically. Plummeting oil production became the country's leading economic indicator: it plummeted, then the GDP plummeted, then coal and natural gas production plummeted. A decade after its peak, oil production was down 40 percent. Russia's oil production subsequently staged a partial recovery thanks to foreign investment, imported technology and the simple fact that the pause in production following the Soviet collapse gave the oil time to pool around existing wells through capillary action. The inefficiency of Soviet oil production turned out to be its saving grace. Wells had been abandoned as soon as pressure at the wellhead started to fall. A decade after Soviet collapse these same wells could be made to produce again, thanks to better technology.

Entire bookshelves full of books have been devoted to the energy predicament that confronts the United States, there to read for anyone who wants to delve deeply into this seriously depressing subject. Here, I will simply list some of the most salient facts.

The US started out with more oil than Saudi Arabia, but now imports three-quarters of its needs. Oil production in the US peaked in 1970, and has been declining ever since. Globally, conventional oil production peaked in 2005 and all liquid fuel production peaked in 2008. The world currently consumes over four units of oil for each new unit it finds, making any new peaks in global oil production unlikely. Much of the oil comes from aging giant fields, such as Ghawar in Saudi Arabia, Burgan in Kuwait, Cantarell in Mexico and Daquing in China. These giant fields are showing very serious and sudden declines, so that, for example, Mexico will shortly be in no position to continue exporting oil to the US.

Crude oil is and will remain the world's main enabler of industrial activity, because most of the world's transportation infrastructure runs on products derived from it: gasoline, diesel and jet fuel. Even if it could be redesigned to run on something else, the process of replacing it would take decades. It would have to be replaced with items manufactured using the current industrial infrastructure, and this would require a level of industrial activity that can no longer be sustained. The time window for initiating such changes has already closed: the oft-cited Hirsch Report states that it would take twenty years to prepare for Peak Oil in order to avoid a severe and prolonged shortage of transportation fuels. Given that the peak was back in 2005, we now have minus twenty-five years left before we must start preparing. According to Hirsch et al., we have failed to prepare already.

Such is the cost of denial. Even five years ago everyone from government officials to oil company executives treated Peak Oil theory as the work of a lunatic fringe. But now that global Peak Oil has started to come into focus in everyone's rearview mirror, all and sundry are ready to concede that there are serious problems with growing or even maintaining the oil supply. Some people still feel skittish about using the term Peak Oil, but the differences of opinion now largely stem from the refusal to accept the terminology of Peak Oil rather than the substance of peaking global oil production. This is, of course, quite understandable: it must be awkward for oil industry insiders to go from shouting "Peak Oil is bunk!" to shouting "Peak Oil is nigh!"

This does not mean that we are done with denial: not at all! We have simply moved from denying that global Peak Oil is happening to denying that Peak Oil will put an end to economic growth and to most types of industrial activity. The old conventional wisdom that had forecast endless resource growth supporting economic growth far into the future is gradually giving way to an acceptance of gradual decline, where economic activity becomes constrained by oil production, which is expected to decrease by a few percent a year. The theoretical underpinning of this prediction is that while the upward slope of Peak Oil is economically constrained, the downward slope is only constrained by the geology of depleting oil reservoirs and by oil extraction technology, which cannot improve forever without encountering diminishing returns. While the oil supply is growing, oil demand fluctuates, resulting in numerous ups and downs in production superimposed on the overall upward trend as production tries to match demand. But on the downward side, demand permanently exceeds supply, so that every barrel of oil that can be produced at each instant *will* indeed be produced.

Peak Oil theory has been able to provide a reasonably accurate way of predicting the depletion profile of separate countries and provinces. If you look at oil production in the continental United States after its peak in 1970, it does show just such a gradual decline. We are seeing a similar pattern in other past-peak provinces: Britain's North Sea and Indonesia. In these cases, oil production was indeed resource-constrained, and followed the natural depletion profile determined by a combination of geology and technology. But these predictions cannot be extrapolated to the world as a whole, for one very obvious reason: when faced with a domestic production deficit, the countries in question were able to keep their economies functioning by importing oil from countries that still had a production surplus. But once global Peak Oil comes and goes, there will be nowhere left to turn for imports. And when faced with a steadily shrinking oil supply, industrial economies do not steadily shrink: they suddenly implode.

It turns out that, in an industrialized economy, a drop in oil consumption precipitates a proportional drop in overall economic activity, because oil is what enables products and services to be delivered throughout the economy. In the US in particular, there is a very strong correlation between GDP and motor vehicle miles traveled. Thus, the US economy can be said to run on oil, in a rather direct and immediate way: less oil implies a smaller economy. At what point does the economy shrink so much that it can no longer meet its own maintenance requirements? (In order to continue functioning, all sorts of infrastructure, plant and equipment must be maintained and replaced in a timely manner, or it all stops functioning.) Once that point is reached, economic activity becomes constrained not just by the availability of transportation fuels, but also by the availability of serviceable equipment. Also, at what point does the economy shrink so much as to invalidate the financial assumptions on which it is based, making it impossible to continue importing oil on credit? Once that point is reached, the amount of transportation fuel available is no longer limited just by the availability of oil, but also by the inability to finance oil imports.

The initial shortage of transportation fuel need not be large in order to trigger this entire cascade of events, because even a small shortage triggers a number of economically destructive feedback loops. A lot of fuel is wasted by idling in line at the few gas stations that remain open. More fuel is wasted by topping off — keeping the tank as full as possible, not knowing when and where you will be able to fill it again. Even more fuel disappears from the market because people are hoarding it in jerry cans and improvised containers. As the shortages drag on and spread, a black market develops; fuel diverted from official delivery channels and siphoned from gas tanks becomes available on the black market at inflated prices. The effect of even a minor initial shortage can easily snowball into an economic disruption sufficient to push the economy over physical and financial thresholds and toward collapse. These effects can be expected to be particularly explosive in the US, where many people feel that driving their own cars is an inalienable right and, in times of gasoline shortages, tend to bring baseball bats and shotguns to filling stations.

In addition to the untenable central assumption that industrial economies will be able to scale down gracefully, there are many additional considerations that make post-Peak predictions of Peak Oil theory of questionable value.

First, these predictions are based on reserve numbers that have been consistently overstated. Much of the remaining oil is in the Middle East, in OPEC countries, which overstated their reserves by various large amounts during OPEC's "quota wars" back in the 1980s. While other OPEC members sheepishly cooked up bogus numbers that looked vaguely real, Saddam Hussein, who was always a bit of a showboat, rounded up Iraq's reserve numbers up to a nice round number: 100 billion barrels. And so OPEC reserves turn out to have been inflated by some large amount — about a third at a minimum. Nor is OPEC unique in overstating its capacity. Energy companies in the US play much the same game in order to please Wall Street.

Second, there is a phenomenon called Export Land Effect: oil-exporting countries, when their production starts to falter, have a strong tendency to cut exports instead of trying to reign in domestic consumption. To be sure, there are still some countries that have surrendered their resource sovereignty to the few remaining inter-national energy companies and have lost control over their export policies, but after a decade of fierce resource nationalism the national oil companies like Saudi Aramco, Russia's Gazprom and China's CNOC are calling most of the shots worldwide. There are also some despotic regimes that starve their domestic consumers but continue to earn the export revenue they need to prop themselves up. But most countries will only export their surplus production. This means that it will become impossible to buy oil internationally long before all the wells run dry, leaving oil-importing countries out in the cold. This effect will be particularly pronounced in the case of the US, which is almost entirely car-dependent and, unlike certain other oil-importing countries such as China, has declined to enter into long-term production agreements with the governments of oil-exporting countries.

Third, although total quantities of oil produced throughout the world were increasing up until 2005, the amounts of oil-based products (gasoline, diesel, etc.) delivered to their points of use peaked sometime earlier, because it has been taking more and more energy to get a barrel of oil out of the ground. This is measured as EROEI (Energy Returned on Energy Invested), which went from 100:1 at the dawn of the oil age, when a few strong-backed lads could dig you an oil well using picks and shovels, to 10:1, now that oil production requires deepwater platforms (that sometimes blow up and poison entire ecosystems), horizontal drilling and fracturing technology, secondary and tertiary recovery using water and nitrogen injection, oil/water separation plants, and all sorts of other technical complexities which consume more and more of the energy they produce. At some point it will no longer be physically possible to deliver diesel or gasoline to a gas station. When that point comes is not yet certain, but there are some indications that 3:1 is the minimum EROEI that the energy sector requires in order to sustain itself. The effect of decreasing EROEI is to make the gentle slope of post-Peak Oil production decline much steeper.

Fourth, we must consider the fact that our modern global oil industry is highly integrated. If you need a certain specialty part for your drilling operation, chances are it can be sourced from just one or two global companies. Chances are this company has some very important, highly technical operations in a country that just happens to be an oil importer. The significance of this becomes clear when one considers what happens to that company's operations once Export Land Effect becomes felt. Suppose you are a national oil company in an oil-rich nation that still has enough oil left for domestic consumption, although it was recently forced to fire all of its foreign customers. Your oil fields are huge but mature, and you can only keep them in production by continuously drilling new horizontal wells just above the ever-rising water cut and maintaining well pressure by injecting seawater underneath. If you stop or even pause this activity, then your oil, at the wellhead, will quickly change in composition from slightly watery oil to slightly oily water, which you might as well just pump back underground. And now it turns out that the equipment you need to keep drilling horizontal wells comes from one of the unlucky countries that used to import your oil but now cannot, and the technicians who used to build your equipment have given up trying to find enough black-market gasoline to drive to work and are busy digging up their suburban backyards to grow potatoes. A short while later your drilling operations run out of spare parts, your oil production crashes, and most of your remaining reserves are left underground, contributing to an increasingly important reserve category: never-to-be-produced reserves.

Finally, as oil production fails to satisfy demand, we should expect to see price spikes. In addition to other kinds of economic damage, these spikes will drive up the prices of many other commodities, such as steel and cement, which depend on energy, including energy from oil, for their production and transportation. The oil industry consumes prodigious quantities of these energy-dense materials. If the price of oil doubles but the cost of these materials triples in response, then the effect of these higher commodity prices is to make oil production uneconomic even with the higher oil prices. Oil exploration and production are capital-intensive activities that require long-term planning and a stable economic environment, and commodity price spikes disrupt these plans and cause projects to be delayed or canceled, resulting in less oil being produced than would otherwise be expected.

These factors will combine to produce sudden, stepwise declines in the oil supply. They will hit different countries at different times, but we should expect the first victims to be the most highly indebted, most import-dependent, most oil-dependent countries. The canary in that particular coal mine happens to be the United States. The swift disappearance of the US from the international oil market will give a few years of breathing space to the oil-importing nations that are farther away from the edge, giving them time to recognize and adapt to the new reality. However, with any luck, a thriving black market in gasoline will give people in some parts of the US some access to gasoline for a few years longer, at prices that will allow for some uses, such as running an electrical generator at an emergency center (if you decide to stay), or driving as far as the nearest border (if you don't). But there is one thing of which we can be quite sure: that a long and gradual global oil production decline is exceedingly unlikely. Knowing this fact should impart a sense of urgency. If Americans wish to prepare for life without oil, they most likely have a few months, maybe even a few years, but they certainly do not have a few decades. Let those who would have you believe otherwise address all of the issues I have raised here.

Housing

One important element of collapse preparedness is making sure that you do not need a functioning economy to keep a roof over your head. In the Soviet Union, all housing belonged to the government, which made it available directly to the people. Since all housing was also built by the government, it was only built in places that the government could service using public transportation. After the collapse, almost everyone managed to keep their home.

In the Soviet Union, nobody owned their place of residence. This meant that the economy could collapse without causing homelessness: just about everyone went on living in the same place as before. There existed no mechanism to parallel the American practice of evictions or foreclosures. The right to occupy one's assigned place of residence, which was inscribed in one's internal passport, could only be relinquished voluntarily or through death. Everyone stayed put, and this prevented society from disintegrating.

Russia's chronic housing shortage was partly caused by the spectacular decline of Russian agriculture, which caused people to migrate to the cities, and partly by the government's inability to put up buildings quickly enough. What the government wanted to put up was invariably an apartment building: 5 floors, 9 floors, and even some 14-floor towers. The buildings went up on vacant or vacated land and were usually surrounded by a generous portion of wasteland, which, in the smaller cities and towns, and in places where the soil is not frozen year-round, or covered with sulfur or soot from a nearby factory, was quickly converted into kitchen gardens.

The quality of construction always looked a bit shabby but has turned out to be surprisingly sound structurally and quite practical. Mostly it was reinforced concrete slab construction, with ceramic tile on the outside and hard plaster for insulation on the inside. It was cheap to heat, and usually had heat, at least enough of it so that the pipes didn't freeze, with the hot water supplied by a gigantic central boiler that served an entire neighborhood. Since all services, including heat, running water, garbage removal and maintenance were centralized, they were cheap in terms of labor, materials and energy, and this made it possible for them to continue after the collapse, given a minimum of community effort.

One often hears that the shabbiest of these Soviet-era apartment blocks, termed *Khrushcheby* — a melding of Khrushchev, who ordered them built, and *trushcheby* (Russian for "slums") — are about to start collapsing, but they haven't done so yet. Yes, they are dank and dreary, and the apartments are cramped, and the walls are cracked, and the roof often leaks, and the hallways and stairwells are dark and smell of urine — but it's housing.

Because apartments were so hard to come by, with waiting lists stretched out for decades, several generations generally lived together. This was often an unpleasant, stressful and even traumatic way to live, but also very cheap. Grandparents often did a lot of the work of raising children, while the parents worked. When the economy collapsed, it was often the grandparents who took to serious gardening and raised food during the summer months. Working-age people took to experimenting in the black market, with mixed results: some would get lucky and strike it rich, while for others it was lean times. With enough people living together, these accidental disparities tended to even out, at least to some extent.

In the United States, very few people own their place of residence free and clear, and even they need an income to pay real estate taxes. The real owners of real estate in the US are banks and corporations. People without an income face homelessness. When the economy collapses, very few people will continue to have an income, so homelessness will become rampant. Most people in the US, once their savings are depleted, will in due course be forced to live in their car, or in some secluded stretch of woods, in a tent or under a tarp. There is currently no mechanism by which landlords can be made not to evict deadbeat tenants, or banks prevailed upon not to foreclose on nonperforming loans. Recent attempts at government-subsidized loan modification have been less than successful, and have amounted to an effort to help banks by propping up real estate prices rather than to help the population by making housing more affordable. Once enough residential and commercial real estate becomes vacant, and law enforcement becomes lax or nonexistent, squatting becomes a real possibility. Squatters usually find it hard to get mail and other services, but this is a very minor issue. More importantly, they can be easily dislodged again and again.

Given the car-dependent nature of most US suburbs, where over half of the population now lives, we should expect many of them to be abandoned, resulting in mass migrations of homeless people toward the more survivable city centers. By a lucky accident, much of the suburban housing stock is actually of very low intrinsic value, constructed out of a few sticks, a bit of tarpaper and some plastic and cardboard sheets. These American-style Potemkin villages will be simple to knock down. Whereas more solidly constructed buildings might require a few swings with a wrecking ball, the merest touch from a bulldozer will be sufficient to cause these little market bubbles to fold up into a pile of kindling and dust with barely a groan. Suburbia will leave no majestic ruins, and even a post-industrial population of the future will have little trouble reclaiming it as farmland or pasture. One lasting legacy of the suburban experiment will be the proliferation of flooded foundation pits. Many suburban basements have to be kept dry with the help of electric sump pumps and dehumidifiers; when left unattended they quickly turn into little malarial swamps. But once their ticky-tacky superstructure is demolished they can also be used for aquaculture or tree nurseries.

In the more densely built-up areas, we can imagine that the now permanently empty parking garages and parking lots will turn into trailer parks and shantytowns or will be converted to raised bed agriculture, that city parks will be used to grow grain or fodder, and that elevated roadways will be lined with barrels to collect rainwater (which will run clear once industry and transportation have both largely shut down). With little of the old commerce or business continuing to function, much of the commercial real estate, including office towers, may come to be inhabited, although nothing above the tenth floor will be of much use once the elevators stop running.

Even the most commonsense and humble adaptations will present public officials in the US with a terrible choice: enforce property laws or let people die. The US and the Soviet Union were at two extremes of a continuum between the public and the private. In the Soviet Union, most land was open to the public. Even apartments were often communal, meaning that the bedrooms were private but the kitchen, bathroom and hallway were common areas. In the US, most of the land is privately owned, some by people who put up signs threatening to shoot trespassers. Most "public places" are in fact private, marked "Customers Only" and "No Loitering." Where there are public parks, these are often "closed" at night, and anyone trying to spend a night there is likely to be told to "move along" by the police. The term "loitering" does not even translate into Russian. The closest equivalent one can find is something along the lines of "hanging around" or "wasting time" in public. This is important, because once nobody has a job to go to, the two remaining choices are to sit at home or, as it were, to loiter. If loitering is illegal, then staying at home becomes the only choice. If there is no home, then breaking the law becomes the only option.

After the collapse, Russia experienced a swelling of the ranks of people described by the acronym BOMZh, which stands for "persons without a definite place of residence or occupation." The *bomzhies*, as they came to be called, often inhabited unused bits of the urban or rural landscape where, with nobody to tell them to "move along," they were left largely in peace. Such an indefinite place of residence was often referred to as a *bomzhatnik*. English badly needs a term for that. When the US economy collapses, one would expect employment rates and, with them, residency rates, to plummet. It is hard to estimate what percentage of the US population will, as a result, become homeless, but it could be quite high, perhaps becoming so commonplace as to remove the stigma. A country where most neighborhoods are structured so as to exclude people of inadequate means in order to preserve property values is not a pleasant place to be a bum. Then again, when property values start dropping to zero, we may find that some of the properties spontaneously rezone themselves into *bomzhatniks*, with no political will or power anywhere to do anything about them.

I do not mean to imply that Russian bums had a good time of it. But because most Russians were able to keep their place of residence in spite of a collapsing economy, the percentage of *bomzhies* in the general population never made it into the double digits. These most unfortunate cases led short, brutal lives, often in an alcoholic haze, and accounted for quite a lot of Russia's spike in post-collapse mortality. Some of them were refugees — Russians ethnically cleansed from the newly independent, suddenly nationalistic former Soviet republics — who could not be easily reabsorbed into the motherland due to Russia's chronic housing shortage.

The population of the United States has been rather slow to respond to the real estate collapse and foreclosure crisis which has been unfolding for three years now, making it unlikely that necessary changes will be effected in a timely manner to prevent a very large increase in homelessness. The first step would be to abandon certain erroneous and unhelpful notions: that housing is an investment (it is an unproductive asset and a cost); that small single-family suburban dwellings are desirable (they are a tremendously inefficient way to inhabit the landscape); that it is acceptable for rent or mortgage to be a major category of expense (it wastes resources on an unproductive *rentier* class); and finally, that the right to have a place to live, regardless of any economic or financial considerations, should not be viewed as a political right: the right to inhabit your country. But there is little evidence that any of these realizations are even starting to sink in. To be sure, a few families will come up with creative alternatives for themselves (we, for instance, live on a boat). But most citizens of the US seem dead set on becoming that which they almost universally despise: bums.

Transportation

Soviet public transportation was more or less all there was, but there was plenty of it. A typical Russian city has a subway (metro), buses, streetcars (trams) and electric buses (trolleybuses). Cities are connected to their suburbs by electric trains (*elektrichki*) and to other cities by long-distance passenger services featuring a variety of sleeping arrangements, ranging from *platskart* (a live geometric experiment in efficiently packing bodies in three dimensions using multiple tiers of folding cots) to *coupé* (lower population density, affording slightly more privacy using sliding doors) to the luxurious SV (sleeper car). All of this public infrastructure was designed to be almost infinitely maintainable, and continued to run even as the rest of the economy collapsed.

Russian housing is generally accessible by public transportation, which continued to run during the worst of times. Most of the Soviet-era developments were centrally planned and central planners do not like sprawl: it is too difficult and expensive to service. Few people owned cars and even fewer depended on cars for getting around. Even the worst gasoline shortages resulted in only minor inconveniences for most people: in the springtime, they made it difficult to transport seedlings from the city to the dacha for planting; in the fall, they made it difficult to haul the harvest back to the city.

The population of the United States is almost entirely car-dependent, and relies on markets that control oil import, refining and distribution, as well as on continuous public investment in road construction and repair. The cars themselves require a steady stream of imported parts and are not designed to last very long. When these intricately interconnected systems stop functioning, much of the population will find itself stranded. Once cars become inaccessible to a significant portion of the population, not only will this development sound the death knell for the myth of American inclusiveness, but the anger and envy of the automotively dispossessed will quickly make cars an unsafe form of travel for the rest of the population. The resulting environment is likely to run the gamut between what we see in Israel (paramilitary security, high walls and watchtowers, and private roadways for the rich) and what we see in Iraq (endless checkpoints, roadside bombs and armed convoys).

For those of us who do not wish to live and die by the automobile, the challenge is not just one of eliminating cars from our own lives, but of constructing an environment that is sufficiently inhospitable to cars to make their demise a non-event. This challenge cannot be met by printing up bumper stickers and organizing events to which people can drive, effectively placing it outside the scope of American politics. Thus, the coming widespread unavailability of cars has placed American politics outside the scope of reality, and it is only a matter of time before people are forced to notice this particular inconvenient truth. Al Gore's prescription, presented playfully to music at the end of his now famous film, is basically to drive carefully so as not to leave too many carbon footprints. I believe this rather misses the point. What are you supposed to do with your last tank of gas? Drive off a cliff slowly, so as to conserve energy?

When it comes to holding the country together in the post-petroleum age, the US has left itself very few viable options. Without a concerted effort to rebuild transcontinental railroad links prior to the onset of crisis conditions, once the remaining airlines go bankrupt and the pavement on interstate highways reverts to dirt, the two coasts will remain connected by the Panama Canal only, forcing them to part company. There is no evidence that such an effort is even being considered. Navigable rivers and canals will once again start serving a vital function, determining which population centers remain in communication with the rest of the world, the rest becoming largely isolated. The canal system remains for the most part intact, and building barges is a low-tech proposition, achievable using hand tools and reclaimed materials, even in the midst of an economic standstill. Many towns have partially abandoned waterfronts, which have been supplanted, first by the railheads, then by the highways and the airports. These can surely be put to good use.

The most successful form of transportation by far is the bicycle. While there is currently a bicycle for almost every person in the US, these bicycles by and large sit still in garages and basements, rusting and gathering dust. About a tenth of them might be rideable at any given time. If large numbers of people attempt to start using them, the immediate effect will be a shortage of bicycle tires, which deteriorate due to dry rot. Even if this problem finds a solution, it will soon be discovered that the vast majority of the bicycles are in fact toys designed for sport, not for hauling loads or for the rigors of a daily commute, and most of them will fail within a year of hard daily use. Overhauling them requires a wide assortment of imported spare parts, which is unlikely to be available. The old three-speed Columbias and other antiques, which were designed to carry 300 pounds and to go 100,000 miles between overhauls, will suddenly become highly prized. Many other bikes will still be used, even if they are no longer rideable, as push-bikes, Ho Chi Minh Trail style: they will be walked instead of ridden, with one stick shoved down the seat-post, another tied to the handlebar and heavy loads slung in bags over the top tube.

Shopping carts, released en masse from the confines of defunct shopping areas, can be expected to proliferate wildly. They are already abundant: I once counted over a dozen in the course of a short walk through the woods on the banks of the Charles River just west of Boston, rusting peacefully on the riverbank. Shopping carts are ugly, noisy and unreliable, but they are also an obvious fallback for a population that has lost all access to transportation: they are plentiful, their operation and maintenance should not present much of a learning curve to the general population and everyone who wants one seems to be able to get one.

Employment

Economic collapse affects public sector employment almost as much as private sector employment — eventually. Because government bureaucracies tend to be slow to act, they collapse more slowly. Also, because state-owned enterprises tend to be inefficient and stockpile inventory, there is plenty of it left over for the employees to take home and use in barter. Most Soviet employment was in the public sector and this gave people some time to think about what to do next. Private enterprises tend to be much more efficient at many things, such as laying off their staff, shutting their doors and liquidating their assets. Since most employment in the United States is in the private sector, we should expect the transition to permanent unemployment to be quite abrupt for most people.

A spontaneous soft landing is unlikely in the US, where a large company can decide to shut its doors by executive decision, laying off personnel and auctioning off capital equipment and inventory. Since in many cases the equipment is leased and the inventory is just-in-time and therefore very thin, a business can be made to evaporate virtually overnight. And because many executives may decide to cut their losses all at once, seeing the same economic projections and interpreting them similarly, the effect on communities could be utterly devastating.

While the US economy is supremely efficient at destroying jobs, and has succeeded, over the past decade, in creating an entire new class of people, almost twenty million strong, who are either permanently unemployed or underemployed, it is far less effective in creating jobs. Actually, it can create jobs just fine — just not in the US. It seems that nobody particularly wants to hire Americans, and so China, India and other rapidly developing nations have been the beneficiaries of US government stimulus programs designed to create jobs. It's a rational choice: Americans have high medical costs (they are fat and sickly because of a bad diet, a sedentary lifestyle and a predatory medical system), have high transportation costs (since so many of them drive around in empty trucks and buses), pay a lot in utilities (since so many of them choose to live in houses that are big enough to house entire Chinese villages) and generally require a high salary just to live badly. This arrangement has been good for corporate profits, so far, although killing your customers is not a great long-term policy. The corporations exist to maximize value for their shareholders, not to serve their employees or the public at large, but even if their mission was to maximize global happiness, the result would be the same: Why employ one economically insecure, underpaid, disgruntled American when you can employ ten suddenly prosperous and immensely satisfied Chinese or Indians for the same amount? It is simply more efficient to spend economic stimulus money abroad than in the US.

But when collapse is staring you in the face, the one thing you don't want to do is to collapse efficiently, and this is an area where the citizens of the former Soviet Union gathered quite a windfall. The Soviet centrally planned behemoth was extremely inefficient, with high levels of loss and outright waste at every level. The distribution system was so inflexible that enterprises hoarded inventory. It excelled at producing capital goods, but when it came to manufacturing consumer goods, which require much more flexibility than a centrally planned system can provide, it failed miserably. It also failed miserably at producing food, especially high-protein food such as meat and poultry, and was forced to resort to importing many basic foodstuffs. It operated a huge military and political empire but, paradoxically, failed to derive any economic benefit from it, running the entire enterprise at a net loss.

Also paradoxically, these very failings and inefficiencies made for a soft landing. Because there was no mechanism by which state enterprises could go bankrupt, they often continued to operate for a time at some low level, holding back salaries or scaling back production. This lessened the number of instant mass layoffs or outright closings, but where these did occur, they were accompanied by very high mortality rates among men between the ages of 45 and 55, who turn out to be psychologically the most vulnerable to sudden loss of career, and who either drank themselves to death or committed suicide.

People could sometimes use their old, semi-defunct place of employment as a base of operations of sorts, from which to run the kind of black market business that allowed many of them to gradually transition to private enterprise. The inefficient distribution system, and the hoarding to which it gave rise, resulted in very high levels of inventory, which could be bartered. Some enterprises continued to operate in this manner, bartering their leftover inventory with other enterprises in order to supply their employees with something they could use or sell.

What parallels can we draw from this to employment in the post-collapse United States? Public sector employment may provide somewhat better chances for keeping one's job. For instance, it is unlikely that all schools, colleges and universities will dismiss all of their faculty and staff at the same time. Nor will government agencies, government-funded research labs or government contractors involved in support and maintenance activities. It is somewhat more likely that their salaries will not be enough to live on, but they may, for a time, be able to maintain their social niche. Properties and facilities management is probably a safe bet: as long as there are properties that are considered valuable, they will need to be looked after. When the time comes to dismantle them and barter off the pieces, it will help if they are still intact, and help you if you are the one who has the keys to them.

But by far the best way to adapt to a situation where there is a large and growing shortage of jobs is to not need one. In a society where most interactions between people — from child care to foot massage — have been commercialized, this sort of adaptation takes time and practice, but it is still possible to draw a distinction between a job and work: jobs are increasingly scarce, but work is always plentiful. A shortage of jobs can be seen as a glut of work — work on projects that allow people to live without spending the money they don't have because they are unemployed. A big kitchen garden and a chicken coop can cut food bills down to where food stamps are enough to cover what can't be grown locally. A knowledge of medicinal herbs, a steadfast refusal to take life too seriously and plenty of physical labor in the open air can help avoid running up medical bills. Knowledge of several trades makes it unnecessary to hire tradesmen to build and maintain what you need. Of course, it is impossible to be completely self-sufficient, and there are situations where other people have to be brought in to help. And then the scarcest resource, it turns out, is not jobs but neighbors who have useful skills and are willing to put them to good use outside of a job. And a plentiful but unclaimed resource turns out to be nut jobs: people who lay awake at night wondering whether someone somewhere has managed to get around them and get what they need without paying for it.

One major difference is that the Soviet Union was entirely self-sufficient when it came to skilled labor. Both before and after the collapse, skilled labor was one of its main exports, along with oil, weapons and industrial machinery. Not so with the United States, where not only is most of the manufacturing being carried out abroad, but a lot of service back home is being provided by immigrants. This runs the gamut from farm labor, landscaping and office cleaning to the professions, such as engineering and medicine, without which society and its infrastructure would unravel. Most of these people came to the United States to enjoy the superior standard of living — for as long as it remains superior. Many of them will eventually head home, leaving a gaping hole in the social fabric.

I have had a chance to observe quite a few companies in the US from the inside and have spotted a certain constancy in the staffing profile. At the top, there is a group of highly compensated senior lunch-eaters. They tend to spend all of their time pleasing each other in various ways, big and small. They often hold advanced degrees in disciplines such as Technical Schmoozing and Relativistic Bean-counting. They are obsessive on the subject of money and cultivate a posh country set atmosphere, even if they are just one generation out of the coal mines. Ask them to solve a technical problem and they will politely demur, often taking the opportunity to flash their wit with a self-deprecating joke or two.

Somewhat further down the hierarchy are the people who actually do the work. They tend to have fewer social graces and communication skills, but they do know how to get things done. Among them are found the technical innovators, who are often the company's raison d'être. More often than not, the senior lunch-eaters at the top are native-born Americans and, more often than not, the ones lower down are either visiting foreigners or immigrants. These find themselves in a variety of situations, from the working visa holders who are often forced to choose between keeping their job and going home, to those who are waiting for a green card and must play their other cards just right, to those who have a green card, to naturalized citizens.

The natives at the top always try to standardize the job descriptions and lower the pay scale of the immigrants at the bottom, playing them against each other, while trying to portray themselves as super-achieving entrepreneurial mavericks who can't be pinned down to a mere set of marketable skills. The opposite is often the case: the natives are often the commodity items, and would perform similar functions whether their business were biotechnology or salted fish, while those who work for them may be unique specialists, doing what has never been done before.

It is no surprise that this situation should have come about. For the last few generations, native-born Americans have preferred disciplines such as law, communications and business administration, while immigrants and foreigners tended to choose the sciences and engineering. All their lives the natives were told to expect prosperity without end, and so they felt safe in joining professions that are mere embroidery on the fabric of an affluent society.

This process became known as the "brain drain" — America's extraction of talent from foreign lands, to its advantage and their detriment. This flow of brain power has already started to reverse direction, with many visiting specialists and recent foreign university graduates going home instead of looking for employment in the US, leaving the country even less capable of finding ways to cope with its economic predicament. This may mean that even in areas where there will be ample scope for innovation and development, such as renewable energy or restoring the rail service, America may find itself without the necessary talent to make it happen.

Families

Russian and American families are in similarly sad shape, with high divorce rates and many out-of-wedlock births. However, women received the right to education and a career in Russia earlier than they did in the US, and there was nothing analogous to the American feminization of poverty, or the ghastly result that two-thirds of American children are born into poverty. Russian single mothers were never victimized to the extent that American single mothers routinely are, and could rely on an array of free social services, from health care to kindergartens, to which they were well and truly entitled. To a large extent, Russian women fought and won the battle for equality a few generations ago. In my own family there was an abrupt, if not to say "revolutionary," transition between my great-grandmother, who was a homebody, a seamstress and a singer (who sung while seated at her Singer) and my grandmother, who was an MD and perfected a technique for identifying cancer cells using UV light and radioactive tracers. By the time the XXI century rolled around, the process of women's liberation from the family and re-enslavement by society had come full circle, to the extent that quite a few talented and educated Russian women came to sport reactionary attitudes: that having a man to take care of you is just dandy; that a job, if one ever becomes necessary, should not be so tiring as to be damaging to one's beauty; and that American feminist attitudes toward gender equality are downright daft.

The commonest cause of domestic strife in Russia was and remains alcoholism. The chronic shortage of housing forced many Russian families to stay together, with mixed consequences. It often resulted in three generations living together under one roof. This didn't make them happy, but at least they were used to each other. The usual expectation was that they would stick it out together, come what may. Another key difference between Russia and the US is that Russians, like most people around the world, generally spend their entire lives living in one place, whereas Americans move around constantly. Not only do most Russians live close to family, but they generally know, or at least recognize, most of the other people who surround them. When the economy collapses, everyone has to confront an unfamiliar situation. The Russians, at least, did not have to confront it in the company of complete strangers. On the other hand, Americans are far more likely than Russians to help out strangers, at least when they have something to spare.

In the United States, families tend to be atomized, spread out over several states. They sometimes have trouble tolerating each other when they come together for Thanksgiving or Christmas, even during the best of times. They might find it difficult to get along in bad times. There is already too much loneliness in this country, and I doubt that economic collapse will cure it.

When confronting hardship, people usually fall back on their families for support. Since for many people in the US this option has been foreclosed by their atomized living arrangement, we need to look to other possibilities. Most surprisingly, Americans make better communists than Russians ever did, or cared to try. They excel at communal living, with plenty of good, stable roommate situations, which compensate for their weak, alienated or nonexistent families. These roommate situations can be used as a template and scaled up to village-sized self-organized communities. Big households that pool their resources make a lot more sense in an unstable, resource-scarce environment than the individualistic approach. Without a functioning economy, a household that consists of a single individual or a nuclear family ceases to be viable, and people are forced to live in ever-larger households, from roommate situations to taking lodgers to doubling up to forming villages. Where any Russian would cringe at such an idea, because it stirs the still fresh memories of the failed Soviet experiment at collectivization and forced communal living, many Americans are adept at making fast friends and getting along and generally seem to possess an untapped reserve of gregariousness, community spirit and civic-minded idealism.

In the US, cheap energy and the giant economic bubble it has fueled have given rise to some social arrangements that are not destined to survive the onset of permanent energy scarcity. One of these is the notion that a few young people will anonymously contribute a large part of their income for the welfare of many old people they have never met or even heard of. For most of human history, parents took care of their children as their topmost priority in life. As with many other species, it was their biological imperative to do so; beyond that, most of them were conscious of the fact that if their children did not survive, neither would they: their genes, their memories, their culture or anything else about them would be erased by time. The care of children could be entrusted to family members but never to complete strangers. The education of children took place largely in the home, through storytelling, shared labor and rites of passage. The elderly, and especially the grandparents, took an active part in rearing and educating children. It was they who watched and attended to young children throughout the day and who inculcated in them much of the ancestral wisdom — the stories, myths and practical knowledge — through ceaseless, tiresome repetition.

At the trailing edge of the fossil fuel age, where the lone remaining superpower now finds itself, prosperous society looks quite different. Both parents work increasingly dismal and time-consuming jobs, mostly away from home, in order to keep themselves out of bankruptcy. Those who prosper most attend to their careers with far greater attention than they attend to their children, abandoning them to the care of strangers for the better part of most days. The grandparents live elsewhere, enjoying their golden years, the fruits of their labors encapsulated in some properties, some investments and a merciful central government that has promised to at least keep them alive if all else fails. They are living on artificial life support that is being scaled back and shut off, one formerly affluent middle-class family at a time.

Once the joy ride ends, human society will revert to norm, but many will suffer and many lives will be cut short. The elderly will get a dose of their own toxic medicine. Adult children will take care of their helpless parents only inasmuch as their parents took care of them when they were young and helpless. Were they placed in day care, sent off to a boarding school, or encouraged to join the military? Well then, institutional care for the elderly must be the perfect solution! (And no use complaining; when their children were three years old and complained, did they listen to them?) Were they made to work for their allowance, to learn the spirit of free enterprise at a young age? Well then, how do their parents expect to earn their keep when they are eighty? Shape up or ship out! These words will not necessarily be said out loud; but they will be felt and lived.

What will make matters worse is that most of the children are humans-"Lite"— deprived of the stories, myths and trials that human children have been put through for the past few million years, minus a bizarre century or two — and so are gravely ill-equipped for life outside the artificial life support system. They are an industrial product: almost from birth they are placed in an entirely artificial social context, where they are evaluated, classified and shoved through a series of institutions, to be readied for a lifetime of service in a system whose feedstock is a commodity human product: Grade A human, marketable skills up-to-date, properly credentialed. Even if their parents and grandparents were intact and able to impart wisdom, the children had not been programmed to process that sort of information.

All that the people in the US can hope for is that strangers will be nice to them. Indeed, there does seem to be a layer of basic decency and niceness to at least some parts of American society, which has been all but destroyed in Russia over the course of Soviet history. There is an altruistic impulse to help strangers and a pride in being helpful to others. In many ways, Americans are culturally homogeneous, and the biggest interpersonal barrier between them is the fear and alienation fostered by their racially and economically segregated living conditions.

On the other hand, there is a streak of sadomasochism running through American political culture that is a mile wide, and a twisted sense of fairness and propriety to go with it. At its root is a primitive idolization of money: the only thing that makes an American good is the goodly quantity of dollars lining his pockets. This is what makes the ritualistic acts of humiliation heaped on the poor and the unfortunate so politically popular even with the very slightly well-to-do; just utter the fashionable term of abuse — "welfare queen" or "illegal immigrant"— and citizens line up in an orderly gamut, ready to dispense corporal punishment.

The two most important social institutions within the US are the individual and the nuclear family, and neither is designed to survive economic collapse. By default, you are a tribe of one, and solitary tribesmen don't tend to do particularly well. It may be beneficial for you to find ways to become significantly more tribal while it is still easy to move around and meet new people.

Money

In the Soviet Union, very little could be obtained for money. It was treated as tokens rather than wealth, and was shared among friends. Many things — housing and transportation among them — were either free or almost free. Since money was not particularly useful in the Soviet economy, and did not directly convey status or success, it was not particularly prized either, and was shared rather freely. Friends thought nothing of helping each other out in times of need. It was important that everyone had some, not that one had more than the others. With the arrival of market economics, this cultural trait disappeared, but it persisted long enough to help people survive the transition.

Most people in the United States cannot survive very long without an income. This may sound curious to some people in the US: How can anyone, anywhere survive without an income? Well, in post-collapse Russia, if you didn't pay rent or utilities (because no one else was paying them either), and if you grew or gathered a bit of your own food, and you had some friends and relatives to help you out, then an income was not a prerequisite for survival.

To keep evil at bay, Americans require money. In an economic collapse, there is usually hyperinflation, which wipes out savings. There is also widespread unemployment, which wipes out incomes. The result is a population that is largely penniless. Beyond the inconveniences associated with having zero disposable income, there is a fantastic social stigma attached to being broke, although an ever-growing group of people in the US gets along quite well without much money at all, and many more could do the same. The list includes pensioners on small fixed incomes, the disabled and those on public assistance. As of 2010, fully 60 percent of Americans receive some form of public assistance. There is also a growing group of conscientious economic underachievers and various categories of the creatively underemployed, such as adult children dwelling in their parents' garages or basements, although, now that circumstances are forcing two-thirds of graduating college seniors to move back in with their parents, this choice no longer seems particularly creative. Many others avoid having to pay rent by housesitting, camping or living aboard boats. But the toxic social environment makes it a sad way to live. The penniless are forcefully prevented from enjoying their freedom from economic necessity, and only the very strong-minded ones can endure with their dignity intact. It takes a great deal of skill to be penniless in the US even with the economy still functioning, and producing plenty of surplus stuff available for the asking. Once it shuts down, even those skilled in the art of surviving without money will be at a loss, while most of the rest of the population will be rendered absolutely helpless.

The commonsense approach to reconciling yourself to the prospect of not having any money is to look for ways to survive without needing any. These ways must be as unique, creative and discrete as the people practicing them, because any sufficiently popular trick for getting something for nothing is automatically rendered useless by its very popularity: other people catch on and start charging them money. This approach also neatly solves the associated problem of losing access to products on which to spend money. But should some products still be available, this approach also avoids the problem of convincing people to accept something as worthless as money in exchange for their ever-more-valuable products. Lastly, this approach also offers a solution to crime: the best way to avoid getting robbed is to have nothing worth stealing. However, instead of concentrating on this commonsense approach, a great many people who are aware of the energy predicament and its implications for the US economy prefer to concentrate on a high-risk approach: hoarding valuables. A great deal of discussion is devoted to the subject of what to hoard and where to hoard it. Should it be gold or silver, or land or other resources? And the follow-on question inevitably becomes: What weapons to buy to safeguard all this stuff?

But there is another follow-on question, which is hardly ever asked: How much is this stuff really going to be worth? Currently, the value of money and other tokens of wealth, such as gold coins, is amplified by fossil fuel energy providing a replacement for human and animal labor equivalent to hundreds of personal slaves for each American. Oil is still about the cheapest liquid money can buy, cheaper than milk, cheaper even than bottled water. When this fossil fuel energy is no longer available, no personal slaves will suddenly materialize out of nowhere and be willing to work for a few pennies a day, because these pennies, in turn, will buy nothing. Even assets that might seem perennially useful, such as farmland, may not make too much sense if it is your own two hands that have to make it productive. Without tractors or combines, irrigation pumps, fertilizers, pesticides and trucks to get the produce to market, a big farm is just a patch of fallow land. Anything beyond a dozen acres may well become just another stranded asset.

If life without money is to become normal for most people in the US, then it seems inevitable that the flow of humanity will become bifurcated. Those who are most helpless will find themselves on the inside, in institutional settings such as jails, asylums and hastily organized camps for the internally displaced, kept alive while the institutions hold together and supplies last. Those who are more resourceful will find ways to remain on the outside, and may find themselves pursued and persecuted as terrorists, while the institutions hold together and supplies last, but eventually they will be left alone as the supplies needed to continue persecuting them run low. Some clever people are sure to find ways to work as conduits between the two worlds, living undercover among the outsiders to obtain intelligence for their institutional masters, but really just looking out for themselves and their friends, and conveying people and supplies back and forth.

For those who want to preserve their wealth, all we can do is wish them good luck. The best that can be accomplished is to lose your wealth slowly over time rather than all at once in a single financial spasm. For those who have any savings at all, a practical approach is to convert paper wealth into physically useful supplies and objects that are likely to become scarce once manufacturing and imports shut down. As for the vexing subject of money, it makes sense to have a stash of gold coins somewhere, for very special occasions, such as paying for passage on a ship, or buying a patch of land. It also makes sense to have a stash of silver coins, for paying for everyday things once stacks of hundred-dollar bills become cheaper than cordwood. But most important and valuable is the ability to de-monetize as many necessities as possible, food and shelter especially. These are two things that many people can provide for themselves using their own two hands, without being paid and without paying anyone. And if you are still wondering what to invest in, invest in developing personal relationships with people who have useful skills. As the old Russian saying goes, "Don't have a hundred rubles but do have a hundred friends."

If you are poor but happy in America, and do not wish to make a target of yourself, you have but two choices: to hide the fact that you are poor or hide the fact that you are happy. If you are in need of help from your fellow man the choice becomes a tricky one. You can, of course, grovel miserably. But you can also impersonate an independently wealthy person who is going through a financially awkward moment, because then even poor Americans will volunteer to spend what little they have on you, just to bask in the glow of your financial righteousness.

Consumerism

Soviet consumer products were always an object of derision — refrigerators that kept the house warm as well as the food, and so on. You'd be lucky if you could buy one at all, and it would be up to you to make it work once you got it home. But once you got it to work, it would become a priceless family heirloom, handed down from generation to generation, sturdy, and almost infinitely maintainable. In the United States, you often hear that something "is not worth fixing." This is enough to make a Russian see red. I once heard of an elderly Russian who became irate when a hardware store in Boston wouldn't sell him replacement bed-springs. "People are throwing away perfectly good mattresses, how am I supposed to fix them?" Economic collapse tends to shut down both local production and imports, and so it is vitally important that anything you own wears out slowly and that you can fix it yourself if it breaks. Soviet-made stuff generally wore incredibly hard. The Chinese-made stuff you can get around here — much less so.

A key difference is that in the Soviet Union consumer products were not profitable, but simply a cost to the government. While in the United States consumer spending is the main mechanism for extracting the money paid out in wages back out of the population, in the Soviet Union both the wages and the expenditure of these wages were dwarfed by government expenditures on capital goods. The manufacturing of consumer products was not seen as a way to satisfy consumer demand, but as a way to keep the consumer at bay by rationing supply. While this can hardly be regarded as an altogether successful scheme, it did have one accidental side benefit: without the profit motive, there was no incentive to make products with an artificially short replacement cycle — planned obsolescence. No effort was expended on researching ways to make products that are useable, but only for a certain duration. The result was a stock of utilitarian and easily repairable consumer items that were sufficiently durable to go on functioning long after they were no longer being manufactured.

In comparison, with the profit motive present and sacrosanct, the United States has a flourishing consumer goods sector. However, it suffers from several fundamental flaws. One of these flaws is that making a new type of long-lasting product normally spells disaster for the manufacturer: once enough of the product has been sold, the market for it can remain saturated for decades, with only a trickle of new sales. Manufacturers employ several tricks to escape this predicament and to shift as much of their product line as possible to what amounts to a rent-based revenue model.

One standard trick is to make the product disposable, forcing consumers to pay for each use. Another is to make the product out of materials that decay at a carefully predetermined rate. Plastics offer excellent possibilities for this sort of fine-tuning: they degrade over time, becoming brittle. This is especially the case for items used out of doors, which suffer photodegradation from the sun's ultraviolet rays. Once a plastic component breaks, it can rarely be mended or replaced with a handmade piece and must usually be replaced with a matching, mass-produced part. Manufacturers also have the option of refusing to sell new parts, instead forcing consumers to "upgrade" to a new, more expensive model. It is often sufficient to replace just one metal part with a plastic one to curtail the lifespan of the overall product. For example, bicycle derailleurs now commonly feature a plastic bracket, ostensibly shaving off an insignificant amount in weight, but capping their lifespan at about ten years.

The pernicious result of this approach in times of economic disruption is obvious: as the flow of products is curtailed, disposable products simply vanish. After an initial period of hoarding, they become available sporadically and in small quantities, but are now treated carefully and reused as much as possible. Disposable cups, plates, bags, syringes, shavers and countless other items suddenly become far less disposable, immersing everyone in a world of increasingly useless, half-broken post-consumer trash. An old-fashioned straight shaver, or a stainless steel-and-glass syringe, suddenly become prized possessions.

This would be a dramatic cultural reversal for a nation accustomed to worshiping at the altar of the new. For decades now, the main thrust of marketing has been to convince everyone that new is better than old, all the while witnessing a steady degradation in the quality of many items. Taking the case of furniture as an example, it has evolved from solid hardwood to softwood with a hardwood veneer, to particleboard with a hardwood veneer, to particleboard with a faux-woodgrain plastic veneer. While solid hardwood furniture can be sanded down and refinished, making it as good as new, the cult of the new forces people to throw it out and then pay for a new, shoddy, disposable, but new-looking replacement. Over the years, I have consistently been able to trash-pick better furniture than I could buy new, while the overall quality of the trash has also gone down continually. At present, most of the trash I see, even in prosperous neighborhoods, is simply appallingly bad and not worth picking.

Another way of making consumers dependent on a continuous flow of new products is through the use of fashion. Here the goal is to make products that are ugly, while simultaneously convincing consumers that a certain kind of ugly is "in" this year. Next year, a subtly different kind of ugliness reigns supreme, while the previous year's ugliness is simply that — ugly, and therefore no longer desirable. The combination of teenage rebellion, adolescent conformism and plain immature silliness offers particularly fertile ground for this type of mass uglification. The result is, again, obvious: when the flow of fashionably ugly new products stops, the products that remain are just plain ugly, and the self-esteem of those who are forced to use them rather low.

Once the consumer has been properly addled into accepting a continuous flow of disposable, shoddy, instantly obsolete products, the next obvious profit-seeking step is to lock up this state of affairs within a financial arrangement based on debt. The two-pronged approach involves outsourcing production to countries with cheap labor and spare energy resources, while providing domestic consumers with access to consumer credit to make up for the shortfall in wages from the lost manufacturing jobs. This puts both the country, and the consumer within the country, permanently in debt. To service this debt, consumers must work ever harder while consuming ever less: an arrangement over which Soviet central planners would surely have salivated profusely.

The last act in the American consumerist tragedy will end with the now naked consumer standing on top of a giant mound of plastic trash. At the end of an economy where everything is disposable stands the disposable consumer. But once the consumer is disposed of, who will be left to take him out with the trash?

Food

The inability to feed their people stands as the Soviet Union's most striking failure. In just a couple of generations, a country that was the breadbasket of Europe had been turned into Europe's agricultural basket case, so that by the time the Soviet Union collapsed it was financially and politically hamstrung by its need to obtain grain import credits from countries that were hostile to its interests. In the 1970s, an oil boom made it complacent, but when the boom ended and oil prices collapsed it was left with no room to maneuver. Its oil provinces reached their all-time peak of production in the mid-80s; consequently, it was unable to further ramp up production and boost exports.

How does a country with more arable land than just about any other, an ancient and successful agricultural tradition complete with all-you-can-eat food festivals and a history of grain surpluses, produce such a dismal result? A short excursion into Russian history might be instructive here: small mishaps can be produced accidentally, but disasters on this scale take serious effort. Speaking of agricultural disasters as a class, it is worth noting at the outset that agriculture is seriously dull work, best done by decidedly simple people who do not mind bending down to touch the ground all day until they look like hunchbacks. Almost genetically predisposed to growing food, these hunchbacks are to be found in all traditional farming societies the world over. As they toil, they wear out the soil very slowly or, if they are not too stressed, and just a bit clever, not at all. In return for their humble servitude, they stay in daily and direct contact with nature in all of its fickle bounty, remaining part of it. As long as they do not resort to shortcuts, such as relying on just one plant, be it maize or potato, their numbers fluctuate naturally along with the climate. But try replacing the humble hunchback with a university-trained agronomist, her hoe with a tractor, her bag of heirloom seeds with some mass-produced hybrid and rainfall with an irrigation pump, and you soon find yourself on the road to environmental oblivion. While Russian agriculture presents us with a particularly frightening example, let us not discount American efforts in the same direction: with enough effort at subjugating nature, through chemical farming, genetic manipulation, pumping down non-replenishing aquifers, ethanol production and other weapons of mass desertification, anything is achievable, even starvation, right here in the US.

Up to the middle of the 19th century, the Russian empire operated something vaguely analogous to the plantation system in the old South, with an ever-more-distant, French-speaking nobility presiding over a multitude of illiterate, Russian-speaking serfs. Based on a more humane serfdom rather than outright slavery, it bound peasants to the land, giving the landowner control over its use and nominal responsibility for their welfare. As the 19th century wore on, the imperial throne found the perpetuation of serfdom increasingly embarrassing to its international prestige as a leading European power, and so, in 1861, less than a month before the outbreak of the American Civil War, serfdom was abolished by imperial decree, without any bloodshed and without any serious detriment to agricultural production. Some peasants were gradually able to acquire their own land, and by the early 20th century the more fertile parts of Russia and the Ukraine had many prosperous farming families. Pre-revolutionary Russia was, by all accounts, a well-fed place.

Then came the man-made disaster known as collectivization, the results of which are plainly visible to this day to anyone who travels through rural Russia and the surrounding lands. The epicenter of this disaster is central Russia, and the farther out one travels — to the Baltic states or to Western Ukraine — the less one sees of its enduring devastation. It is as if a series of plagues had swept through the land, leaving poverty and desolation in its wake. Under the revolutionary slogan "All land to the people!" the prosperous farming families were labeled as the class enemy and persecuted. Grain, including seed grain, was confiscated to feed the starving cities. The result was starvation in the countryside and a collapsing rural population. In place of the prosperous family farms, collective farms were organized, once again binding peasants to the land, but without the benefit of the old church-bound feudal traditions. The introduction of mechanized farm machinery, chemical fertilizers, pesticides and "scientific" farming methods did little to forestall the disaster: the best farmers were either dead or had escaped to the cities. Despite much government effort and some wildly creative solutions, such as attempts at broadcasting seeds using rockets, agricultural production never fully recovered, because fixing the problem involved undoing collectivization and this was not politically advisable.

Another thing not politically advisable was neglecting to feed the people. In particular, all areas at all times had to be supplied with bread, which, more than any other staple, was symbolic of the covenant between the Communist government and the subservient masses. Bread riots, which could not be repressed and could only be quelled by a serendipitous delivery of bread, struck fear into the heart of every local Communist functionary. To make such a scenario unlikely, there were local food stockpiles in every city, stocked according to a government allocation scheme, and staples such as bread were almost always available. And while the quality of other government-supplied food was sometimes questionable, the bread was always excellent — a reflection of its symbolic importance.

But the right to be fed did not necessarily extend beyond the basic carbohydrates, especially in the outlying areas. Moscow was always the best-supplied city, with Leningrad a distant second, while in many provincial towns the store shelves were mostly bare except for bread, vodka and a few varieties of canned foods, and whenever some scarce item, such as sausage, suddenly appeared, lines would instantly form until it was sold out. Shopping was rather labor intensive, and involved carrying heavy loads. Sometimes it resembled hunting — stalking that elusive piece of meat lurking behind some store counter.

Shortly before the Soviet Union's collapse, it became known informally that the 10 percent of farmland allocated to kitchen gardens (in meager tenth-of-a-hectare plots) accounted for some 90 percent of domestic food production. During and after the economic collapse, with the government stores quite uncontaminated by food, and often closed altogether, these plots became lifesavers for many families. The summer of 1990 particularly stands out in my mind: it was the summer when we ate nothing but rice (imported), zucchini (grown by us) and fish (from a local lake, caught by some neighbors).

The dismal state of Soviet agriculture turned out to be paradoxically beneficial in fostering a kitchen garden economy, which helped Russians to survive the collapse. Russians always grew some of their own food, and scarcity of high-quality produce in the government stores kept the kitchen garden tradition going during even the more prosperous times of the '60s and the '70s. After the collapse, these kitchen gardens turned out to be lifesavers. What many Russians practiced, either through tradition or by trial and error, or sheer laziness, was in some ways akin to the new organic farming and permaculture techniques. Many productive plots in Russia look like a riot of herbs, vegetables and flowers growing in wild profusion. In the waning years of the Soviet era, kitchen gardens continued to gain in importance. Beyond underscoring the gross inadequacies of Soviet-style command and control industrial agriculture, their success is indicative of a general fact: agriculture is far more efficient when it is carried out on a small scale, using manual labor.

While most families cooked and ate at home, institutional fare was also considered important. With salaries regulated and with nothing interesting to spend them on, how well fed one was at work took on added significance. Institutional food varied in quality: officers in the nuclear navy ate remarkably well, while privates in the infantry were fed unremarkable porridge and soup. Jobs at many government organizations, factories and institutes were valued for the quality of their commissaries. These sometimes stayed open even as the economy crumbled, production lines stood still and salaries went unpaid for months, providing an important lifeline. Some factory cafeterias even went beyond providing a hot meal; there, workers could buy a whole uncooked chicken or scarce canned goods, all at very reasonable prices.

Restaurants did exist, but were generally outside the budgetary constraints of most families. They always struck me as rather odd, because their menus were by and large works of fiction. Whatever it was you tried to order, the waitress would invariably respond with a laconic "*Nyetu!*" ("We don't have that"). After a few attempts at ordering something you might actually want, you would break down and ask: "What *do* you have?" The answer to this mystery would be something like "Borscht. It's good today." Surprisingly enough, it often was quite good. Although restaurants were something of a rarity, there were always plenty of snack bars, ice cream parlors and refreshment stands.

In addition to small-scale farming, forests in Russia have always been used as an important additional source of food. Russians recognize and eat just about every edible mushroom variety and all of the edible berries. During the peak mushroom season, which is generally in the fall, forests are overrun with mushroom pickers. The mushrooms are either pickled or dried and stored, and often last throughout the winter.

In spite of the monumental failures of Soviet agriculture, the overall structure of Soviet-style food delivery proved to be paradoxically resilient in the face of economic collapse and disruption. The combination of local food stockpiles administered by politicians conditioned to treat bread riots as career-ending calamities, the prevalence of government institutions that attended to the sustenance of their employees and plenty of kitchen gardens, meant that there was no starvation and very little malnutrition. But will fate be as kind to the United States?

Most Americans get their food from a supermarket, which is supplied from far away using refrigerated diesel trucks, making them entirely dependent on the widespread availability of transportation fuels and the continued maintenance of the interstate highway system. In an energy-scarce world, neither of these is a given. Most supermarket chains have just a few days' worth of food in their inventory, relying on advanced logistical planning and just-in-time delivery to meet demand. Thus, in many places, food supply problems are almost guaranteed to develop. When they do, no local authority is in a position to exercise control over the situation and the problem is handed over to federal emergency management authorities. Based on their performance after Hurricane Katrina, these authorities are not only manifestly incompetent, but also appear to be ruled by the ethos that it is better for the government to deny services than provide them, to avoid creating a population that is dependent on government help.

Many people in the United States don't even bother to shop and just eat fast food. The drive to maximize profit while minimizing costs has resulted in a product that manipulates the senses into accepting as edible something that is mainly a waste product. Under strict process control procedures, agro-industrial wastes, sugar, fat and salt are combined into an appealing presentation, packaged, and reinforced by vigorous advertising. Once accepted, it beguiles the senses by its reliable consistency, creating a lifelong addiction to bad food. The chemical industry obliges with an array of deodorants to mask the sickly body odor such a diet produces. Immersed for a lifetime in a field of artificial sensory perceptions, dominated by industrial, man-made tastes and smells, people recoil in shock when confronted with something natural, be it a simple piece of boiled chicken liver or the smell of a healthy human body. Perversely, they do not mind car exhaust and actually like the carcinogenic "new car smell" of vinyl upholstery.

When people do cook, they rarely cook from scratch, but simply re-heat prepackaged factory-produced meals. When they do cook from scratch, the supposedly fresh ingredients come from thousands of miles away and are selected for durability during shipping and long shelf life rather than any actually desirable qualities, making them woody or pulpy and only barely edible. Since good taste is no longer on the menu, the focus shifts to quantity, resulting in appallingly sized portions of undifferentiated protein and starch drowned in fat, administered in national festivals of pathetic gorging, of which Thanksgiving leads the way. But this is all good for business and keeps the cancer, diabetes and heart disease industries humming.

This is all very unhealthy, and the effect on the nation's girth is visible clear across the parking lot. Many of the men have large saggy "man-breasts." Women are deemed sexy in spite of a "muffin-top" (a roll of fat quivering over tight pants) or a "mushroom-cloud" (a similar effect achieved with an overstuffed brassiere). Both men and women proudly display an anatomical innovation called "guttocks": an entire auxiliary derrière worn out front. So pervasive has obesity become in the US that obese people no longer even realize that there is anything wrong with them. To a European, an Asian or an African they look slovenly, weak-willed, unsightly and unwell, but they think that they are just fine. A lot of these people, who just waddle to and from their cars, might seem just the tiniest bit unprepared for what is coming up next. If they suddenly had to start living like Russians they would blow out their knees. Most of them would not even try, but simply wait, patiently or impatiently, for someone to come and feed them. And if that food arrives and consists of a styrofoam box containing a puck of pseudo-meat between two pucks of pseudo-bread and a plastic bottle of water laced with pseudo-syrup, they would be satisfied.

But the food may never arrive. There is already a fair amount of hunger in the United States and many families are forced to choose between food and gasoline. Gasoline is the greater of the two necessities, because they need it to drive to buy food: their car always gets to eat first. In the future, the choice will be made for them: they will be priced out of the market, their food used to produce ethanol, so that the more fortunate can keep driving their cars a tiny bit longer. The process of starving them out might go by one of the euphemistic terms economists seem to favor, such as the somewhat sinister "demand destruction," or the more bland "load shedding." This process is already underway in Mexico, where corn masa producers who provide a staple purchased by the poor are being squeezed out by ethanol producers. The United States is next. Who is that skeleton driving a pickup truck? Let us hope it is not you, but someone else — someone less fortunate than you, with whom you are not acquainted.

But if you are fit of body and sound of mind there is no need to remain a member of this sorry club. Those who have spent some time looking into the viability of local, small-scale agriculture have come up with some results that give us every reason to be optimistic regarding our ability to feed ourselves through our individual and neighborhood efforts, even as the systems of large-scale, industrial agriculture and food delivery unravel due to a combination of high input costs, epic droughts, floods and other freak weather brought on by accelerating climate change, and a shortage of credit caused by the financial collapse. According to Dr. Leonid Sharashkin, who bases his findings on original field research as well as on Russian government data, "Russian households (inclusive of both urban and rural) collectively grow 92% of the country's potatoes on their garden-plots, the size of which is typically 600 square meters (0.15 acres) for urban households, and typically no more than 2500 square meters (0.62 acres) for rural households." And this is Russia, where the potato is a staple carbohydrate along with bread, the growing season is short, the soil is poor, there is often a drought in the spring, and frosts start in August. In most parts of the United States, growing your own food is, comparatively speaking, like falling off a log. The challenge is to start doing so quickly enough.

Medicine

The Soviet government threw resources at immunization programs, infectious disease control and basic care. It directly operated a system of state-owned clinics, hospitals and sanatoriums. Many endemic and epidemic diseases, such as smallpox and polio, were eliminated through aggressive immunization programs. Others, such as tuberculosis, were kept in check. People with fatal ailments or chronic conditions often had reason to complain and had to pay for private care — if they had the money. But access to medical care was guaranteed for everyone. People managed to live out their years not worrying too much about finding a doctor if they needed one. Nor did the Soviet medical system make people sick from worrying about it, put them in debt or leave them to die if they could not pay for treatment.

Perhaps the one truly evil part of the Soviet medical establishment was the system of psychiatric imprisonment, which treated political dissent with aggressive regimens of antipsychotic drugs. The United States is only now starting to catch up in this area, but has already produced some stunning innovations, such as the psychiatric imprisonment of children, where misbehaving adolescents are taken from their families against their families' wishes and committed to mental hospitals. Some of these children are even subjected to aggressive regimens of antipsychotic medications that have not been approved for general use but are provided by pharmaceutical companies for experimental purposes. There is also an effort to redefine teenage rebellion as a psychiatric condition requiring compulsory medication. One of the diagnostic criteria is "disrespect of adult authority." In my capacity as an adult authority (quite accustomed to getting no respect from teenagers) I would like to express the hope that the drugs are just the usual placebos with strange side effects (such as lactation), and that this condition remains chronic, endemic and highly contagious.

Since the dissolution of the Soviet Union, Russian medicine has been largely privatized, with disastrous consequences for public health. It is still possible to be admitted to a hospital without being forced to pay, but once there, the patient may languish without treatment until funds arrive. A childhood friend of mine landed in a provincial hospital after a bad car accident, which left him first unconscious, then disoriented. And there he remained, more or less ignored, until an influential friend accidentally found him there. Shocked by what he saw, the friend walked into the chief surgeon's office, took out his gun, placed it on the surgeon's desk and asked for a very thorough explanation. "Oh, so you want us to treat him?" was the startled response.

While the collapse of the Soviet Union was an abrupt, seismic event, the dissolution of its medical system took the better part of a decade. Surgeons continued to operate, hospitals and neighborhood clinics stayed open, children continued to be immunized and trauma victims continued to be patched up and reanimated. Periodically, desperate pleas could be heard from various dark corners of the former empire, asking for life-preserving drugs to be sent, heart medications especially; eventually these pleas could be heard no more. The weakened system of public health has been unable to check the spread of AIDS, while Russian prisons became incubators for new strains of drug-resistant tuberculosis. At the other extreme, the Russian middle class can generally afford to pay for medical treatment and luxurious clinics offer all manner of special services to those with deep pockets.

Soviet-style medical care is still being practiced in Cuba and, thanks to Cuban medics, in many other countries, especially around the Caribbean. Cuban medics stayed behind in Pakistan and Haiti to treat earthquake victims after the journalists left and Western rescue teams departed in haste. Motivated by an ethos of public service rather than profit, they make a positive difference for many lives. In Belize, which is quite a poor country, I received prompt and excellent free emergency medical care from one such Cuban medic. In the US, in similar circumstances, I had to wait eight hours in an emergency room, then was seen for five minutes by a sleep-deprived intern who scribbled out a prescription for something that is available without a prescription almost everywhere else in the world. Then there ensued a paper battle between the hospital and the insurance company, lasting many months, over whether the hospital could charge for a doctor's visit on top of the emergency room visit. Apparently, doctors are optional in US emergency rooms.

In the United States, medicine is for profit. People seem to think nothing of this fact. There are really very few fields of endeavor to which Americans would deny the profit motive. It could be said that making a profit off the suffering of sick people is simply unethical: it comes down to exploiting the helpless — a predatory practice that a civilized society cannot tolerate. One could hold forth in thunderous condemnation of the political establishment, which, having colluded with the medical-industrial complex, refuses to abide by the people's manifest will to have a reasonable public health care system. Spurious claims to this being a particularly civilized nation aside, the practical problem is that, once the economy is removed, so is the profit, along with the services it once helped to motivate. The result is instantly sky-high rates of morbidity and mortality and a die-off among the most vulnerable: the chronically ill, the elderly and children.

For-profit medicine is an institution of highly questionable merit. The additional nonsensical twist of health insurance, which is only affordable to those who have a permanent, full-time job, makes it a powerful tool of social tyranny. Those without health insurance are a single accident away from losing their savings, their possessions and being saddled with debt they will never be able to repay no matter how hard they work. Medical bills are the leading cause of personal bankruptcy in the US. The fear of this nightmare scenario keeps people securely bound to their jobs. This means that Americans are either in a job they are not at liberty to quit, which is a form of indentured servitude, or are one accident away from becoming slaves to their medical debt, which is another form of indentured servitude. Worry over medical payments is a rising cause of illness in the United States. Doctors, in concert with pharmaceutical companies, reinforce this system of medical enslavement by prescribing, as often as they can, regimens of drugs rather than courses of treatment. They favor new, patented medications, from which the pharmaceutical companies can make the most money. A case in point is antidepressants: these are often prescribed to people who have an objective reason for feeling depressed, but instead of consulting them to change their lives to be less depression-inducing, doctors prescribe dangerous and often ineffectual palliatives. A vicious cycle is created: a job causes depression, a drug enables a person to stay in the job and the job makes it possible to continue receiving the drug. The doctor who perpetuates this vicious cycle is trapped in a vicious cycle of her own, forced to stay within the system in order to make payments against the mountain of student loans accumulated during medical school.

For a long time politicians in the United States have been paying lip service to something they refer to as universal health coverage. What they mean by this is federal legislation to force people to buy private health insurance whether they can afford to or not, and to penalize them for failing to do so. Their goal is not to improve access to health care, but to make free care for the indigent — something their friends in the medical industry dislike — a thing of the past. But the actual concept of insuring someone's health is itself preposterous. Insurance applies to rare, unforeseen events, such as fires or floods, not events that are guaranteed to occur to everyone, such as sickness and death. (Life insurance is an exceptional case of insuring others against the risk of one's premature death.) If all houses eventually burned down, there would be no fire insurance, just as there is no flood insurance for houses in a flood zone. But everybody dies, and nobody dies healthy, and so health insurance is just a way to demand advance payments from people who are still healthy. This allows the medical system to lavish care on the terminally ill while neglecting prevention.

Further, health insurance is bad for your health: in a situation where basic treatment is always provided unconditionally, but chronic or fatal conditions are given as much attention as society can afford, people make an effort to stay healthy. If their treatment for a possibly self-inflicted condition is insured, they lack the strong incentive to avoid risky behaviors or lifestyles. Lastly, health insurance largely reduces the scope of making policy decisions regarding the feasibility of continuing to provide medical care to a financial consideration. If the imperative is for medicine to conquer death, then the financial burden of such a medical system is infinite. With health insurance, the imperative becomes to keep someone alive until the money runs out. Given an increasingly sick and aging population, this arrangement has no future, and any expert on the future of Medicare will tell you that it cannot be paid for.

Given this situation, there is not much that someone who does not wish to wallow in wage slavery can reasonably do. For those with some money, catastrophic health insurance with a very high deductible, plus at least the amount of the deductible tucked away somewhere, can afford some protection in case of accidents. For everyone, staying healthy through good habits, a healthy amount of manual labor, avoidance of stress, overwork, packaged food, polluted places and vicious people is, of course, always advisable. Medical evacuation to a country with a more reasonable health care system should not be neglected as a viable option. Lastly, staying away from doctors, and especially from hospitals, seems advisable: many people die from medications prescribed by doctors, while hospitals spread disease, including drug-resistant bacteria. For those who have or foresee significant ongoing medical needs, staying in the United States will pose a unique set of problems; they might wish to consider seeking refuge in one of the many countries that provides free basic and emergency medical care to their entire population. When it comes to medicine, almost any country in the world will be better than one that is full up with unemployed medical specialists, insurance consultants and medical billing experts.

Education

The Soviet education system was generally quite excellent. It produced an overwhelmingly literate population and many great specialists. Education was free at all levels, but higher education sometimes paid a stipend and often provided room and board. The educational system held together quite well after the economy collapsed. The problem was that the graduates had no jobs to look forward to upon graduation. Many of them lost their way.

As with most things Soviet, education was centrally organized with curriculum set and textbooks approved by Moscow. The schools served the neighborhoods in which they were located and most pupils walked to school, although some used public transportation. The teaching style was decidedly old-fashioned. Standardized tests were unheard of. Grades were issued based largely on oral exams: when called, the pupil stood up and recited the lesson before the class or came up to the blackboard and worked out a problem. Alien inventions such as standardized tests, grading on a curve, varsity sports or the prom, were, obviously, unheard of: school was about learning. But there were usually some club activities available after hours: woodworking or chess, for instance. The pressure to learn was enforced rather simply: not learning was never an option. Pupils who were held back a grade were automatically stigmatized. Because pupils move through the grades as a group (I was in Group B), being held back a grade means having to join another group, made up of younger but already more successful children. Those who were expelled were automatically enrolled in boarding schools, which had much stricter discipline. Those who could not pass the exams to go on to ninth and tenth grade would be transferred to a trade school or enlisted in the army. Those who did succeed in completing all ten grades tried their best to go on to higher education — an institute or a university — by hiring private tutors and by submitting to entrance exams, which were, once again, oral exams before a committee. If accepted, they received room, board and stipend, and, at least prior to the collapse, guaranteed employment after graduation. If not accepted, they were, once again, drafted into the army.

Public primary and secondary education in the US fails to achieve in twelve years what Soviet schools generally achieved in eight. I am sure that this failure can be attributed to many factors: a diet of sugar-water and junk food, many hours of mind-destroying television and video games, the sensory deprivation of the suburban environment and car society, the atomized nature of American society, the underpaid schoolteachers, the nonsense of standardized testing and so forth. Those with plenty of spare time should feel free to ponder such factors, but a much simpler explanation should suffice: American schools fail to educate because that is not their function. Their function is to institutionalize children at an early age. In due course, they will go on to other institutions: jails, psychiatric hospitals, the military or, for those who learn obedience while retaining some semblance of sanity, colleges and universities. There is a reason why jails, hospitals and schools are often architecturally indistinguishable: they are but different parts of the same system, representing different phases of the institutionalization life cycle.

I can offer my own experience with the two educational systems to illustrate the difference between Soviet and American public education. With six incomplete grades of lackluster academic performance at a Leningrad school behind me, I arrived in the US. Here, I was enrolled in the eighth grade. I was always much more interested in languages, history and social studies than in math or science, and so I did my best to avoid learning any more math. This turned out to be surprisingly easy, and, thanks to my six grades of Russian math, I coasted to graduation with similar, consistently lackluster results. After graduation, I continued to coast along, finding that computer work offered the easiest way to make money. But the work turned out to be rather dreary, the long hours kept getting longer (I was automating accounting chores at a major bank and made most of my overtime money compiling quarterly reports), and so I decided that more school wouldn't be any worse. Since I was already up to my neck in computers, I thought that more of the same would not hurt too much and applied. Two local universities accepted me into their computer engineering program and offered me a full scholarship. I enrolled at the one that did not attempt to place me in a remedial math course.

During my consistently lackluster college career, I had to take half a dozen math courses, from Calculus I through Multivariate Calculus, including some applied math courses. Consistently, I did worse than usual when the professor was an American and turned in stellar results if the professor happened to be a Russian (there were, and are, a lot of Russians teaching at this school). This was because the Americans would inevitably try to prep us for taking exams and teach us based on examples of inane, meaningless problems, while the Russians tried to teach us to think based on general principles, presenting each topic in the most general terms possible, sometimes even including some background information on how the particular theoretical point was settled and why on earth it was still being presented to us. Most American students found the Russian approach cruel and unusual. They just wanted to know what was going to be on the midterm and the final and were frustrated by the fact that the professor had not given the question any thought. The exams were sometimes a hilarious train wreck: those who understood the principles, and could demonstrate that they understood them by applying them to any random problem, passed; those who tried to cram for the exam based on homework problems failed miserably. I particularly remember one exam where I could only work out three of the four problems and walked into the professor's office looking rather sheepish. The look I got from him was priceless: I got 75; the passing score was 22.

The higher education system in the United States is good at many things — government and industrial research, team sports, vocational training. But American colleges and universities often fail to achieve in four years what Soviet secondary schools achieved in two (ninth and tenth grades). That is, they fail to produce graduates who have adequate general knowledge, good command of their native language and the ability to acquire specialized knowledge without any further institutional assistance. I am sure that this failure can be attributed to many factors: the star system of professorship, where politically connected faculty members teach seminars on how and why they are glorious, while most of the actual teaching is left up to adjuncts, associate professors, post-docs, teaching fellows and other academic rabble; the dead weight of so-called chips off the old block — children of alumni; the refusal of talented Americans to teach, leaving the field open to foreigners who couldn't get in at home, and so forth. Those with plenty of spare time should feel free to ponder such factors, but again, a much simpler explanation should suffice: the goal of the American higher education system is not to educate.

To me, an educated person is someone free in mind and spirit to explore the universe on their own. Perhaps to you it is just someone who can get a job that pays well; in which case, therein lies your undoing. The American higher education system succeeds brilliantly at one thing: producing a subservient graduate who has no choice but join the labor force on the terms dictated by her future corporate masters. Along with accepting the burden of educational debt, the graduate makes a number of key concessions: that financial success is more important than doing what you want; that having a career is more important than family life; and, perhaps most importantly, that failure is not an option. The newly graduated dentist cannot afford to realize that rotten teeth really freak her out and that she should perhaps do some volunteer work unrelated to dentistry. The need to repay the guaranteed student loans means that she must drill those teeth, whether she wants to or not, while heavily medicated if necessary.

In the United States, higher education is rarely about educating people, in the sense of them learning how to learn, and having the intellectual freedom to do so. It is most commonly about training: the imparting of temporary, quickly obsolescent skills, not universal knowledge. (This, by the way, explains the strange prevalence of adult education and other forms of retraining: the graduates have not been taught how to learn on their own.) But it is mainly about securing unquestioning obedience within a complex rule-following system. The Soviet system required absolute obedience of its educated citizens, but at least some of them were equipped with something called *krugozor*, which English can express only approximately as "a wide mental horizon," and which made them at least theoretically capable of disobedience. The elegant trick of the American higher education system is that the obedience it exacts is automatic: the educated citizens do not know what disobedience would be like, beyond the seemingly pointless, self-defeating refusal to profit from the system, which is really all that they have been taught how to do.

This arrangement may work passably well for the time being, while there is still a system from which they can profit, but it is really a very high price to pay for a bit of vocational training. Twelve years of school plus four years of college is quite a lot of waste, considering that eight years of school and two years of vocational training has been demonstrated to achieve a comparable result. Under the more austere economic regime befitting a bankrupt nation, much of this vainglorious educational infrastructure is bound to fall by the wayside. For those interested in preserving some semblance of civilization on the North American continent, as well as for those who do not wish to push themselves or their children through what will almost certainly amount to a failed program, the emphasis should be on home schooling, apprenticeships and literacy. Illiteracy is already very high in the United States, abnormally high for a developed nation, and it will be a battle to keep this problem from growing much worse. It is definitely a battle worth fighting.

Ethnicity

In terms of racial and ethnic composition, the United States resembles Yugoslavia more than Russia. Ethnically mixed societies are fragile and have a tendency to explode. The social atmosphere of post-collapse America is unlikely to be as placid and amicable as that of post-collapse Russia. At least in parts, it is more likely to resemble other, more ethnically mixed, and therefore less fortunate, parts of the former Soviet Union, such as the Fergana valley (a fertile, densely settled and politically explosive Central Asian valley, shared by Uzbeks, Tajiks, Kyrgyz and other ethnicities) and, of course, that "beacon of freedom" (or so says the US president) in the Caucasus, Georgia.

The United States has traditionally been a very racist country, with numerous categories of people one wouldn't want one's daughter or sister to marry, no matter who one happens to be. It was founded on the exploitation of African slaves and the extermination of the natives. Over its formative years, there was no formal intermarriage between the Europeans and the Africans or the Europeans and the Indians. This stands in stark contrast to other American nations such as Brazil. To this day in the US there remains a disdainful attitude toward any tribe other than the Anglo-Saxon. Glazed over with a layer of political correctness, at least in polite society, this comes out when observing whom most such Anglo-Saxon people actually choose to marry or date.

Russia is a country whose ethnic profile shifts slowly from mainly European in the West to Asian in the East. Russia's settlement of its vast territory was accompanied by intermarriage with every tribe the Russians met on their drive east. One of the formative episodes of Russian history was the Mongol invasion, which resulted in a large infusion of Asian blood into Russian genealogy. On the other side, Russia received quite a few immigrants from Western Europe. Currently, Russia's ethnic problems are limited to combating ethnic mafias and to the many small but humiliating episodes of anti-Semitism, which have been a feature of Russian society for centuries and, in spite of which, Jews, my family included, have done quite well there. Jews were, however, barred from some of the more prestigious universities and institutes and held back in other ways.

The United States remains a powder keg of ethnic tension where urban blacks feel oppressed by suburban whites, who in turn fear to venture into major sections of the cities. In a time of permanent crisis, urban blacks might well riot and loot the cities, because they don't own them, and the suburban whites are likely to get foreclosed out of their "little cabins in the woods," as James Kunstler charmingly calls them, and decamp to a nearby trailer park. Add to this already volatile mixture the facts that firearms are widely available and violence permeates American society, particularly in the South, the West and the dead industrial cities like Detroit.

No part of the United States is an obvious choice for the survival-minded, but some places are obviously riskier than others. Any place with a history of racial or ethnic tension is probably unsafe. This rules out much of the South, the Southwest, and many large cities elsewhere. Some people might find a safe harbor in an ethnically homogeneous enclave of their own kind, while the rest would be well advised to look for the few communities where interethnic relations have been cemented through integrated living and intermarriage and where the strange and fragile entity that is multiethnic society might have a chance of holding together.

Religion

In terms of religion, the Soviet Union was relatively free of apocalyptic doomsday cults. Very few people there wished for a planet-sized atomic fireball to herald the second coming of their savior. This was indeed a blessing.

Pre-revolutionary Russia's two-headed eagle symbolized the monarchy and the church, with a crown on one head and a miter on the other. Along with its somewhat holier manifestations, such as its iconography and monastic tradition, the Russian Orthodox Church was as bloated with wealth and ostentation, and as oppressive, as the monarchy whose power it helped legitimize. But over the course of the 20th century Russia managed to evolve in a distinctly secular way, oppressing religious people with compulsory atheism. The United States, uncharacteristically for a Western nation, remains a deeply religious place, where most people look for and find God in a church, synagogue or mosque. The colonies' precocious move to leave the fold of the British Empire has made the US something of a living fossil in terms of cultural evolution. This is manifested in some trivial ways, such as its refusal to switch to the superior metric system (placing it in company with Liberia and Myanmar) or its distinctly 18th-century tendency to make a fetish of its national flag, as well as in some major ones, such as its rather half-hearted embrace of secularism.

What this difference means in the context of economic collapse is, surprisingly, next to nothing. Perhaps the American is more likely than not to start quoting the Bible and going on about the Apocalypse, the end of times, and the Rapture. These thoughts, need I say, are not conducive to survival. But the supposedly atheist Russian turned out to be just as likely to go on about The End of the World, and flocked to the newly opened churches in search of certainty and solace.

Perhaps the more significant difference is not between prevalence or lack of religion, but the differences between the dominant religions. In spite of the architectural ostentation of the Russian Orthodox Church, and the pomp and circumstance of its rituals, its message has always been one of asceticism as the road to salvation. Salvation is for the poor and the humble, because your rewards are either in this world or the next, not both. This is rather different from Protestantism, the dominant religion in America, which made the dramatic shift to considering wealth as one of God's blessings, ignoring some inconvenient points rather emphatically made by Jesus to the effect that rich people are extremely unlikely to be saved. Conversely, poverty became associated with laziness and vice, robbing poor people of their dignity.

Thus, a Russian is less likely to consider a sudden descent into poverty as a fall from God's grace and economic collapse as God's punishment upon the people, while the religions that dominate America — Protestantism, Judaism and Islam — all feature temporal success of their followers as a key piece of evidence that God is well-disposed toward them. What will happen once God's good will toward them is no longer manifest? Chances are, they will become angry and try to find someone other than their own selves to blame, that being one of the central mechanisms of human psychology. We should look forward to unexpectedly wrathful congregations eager to do the work of an unexpectedly wrathful God.

The United States is by no means homogeneous when it comes to intensity of religious sentiment. When looking for a survivable place to settle, it is probably a good idea to look for a place where religious fervor does not run to extremes.

Inevitable Conclusion

My conclusion is that the Soviet Union was much better prepared for economic collapse than is the United States. America's economy will evaporate like the morning mist. Its population will be stranded wherever they happen to be, and will wait to be rescued. They will expect to be fed, sheltered, defended from each other and told what to do. Many of them will be angry and disoriented and look for someone to blame. Many others know exactly who to blame, and will go on a rampage to avenge age-old injustices.

It is important to understand that the Soviet Union achieved collapse-preparedness inadvertently, and not because of the success of some crash program. Economic collapse has a way of turning economic negatives into positives. The last thing we want is a perfectly functioning, growing, prosperous economy that suddenly collapses one day and leaves everybody in the lurch. Luckily, there is little prospect of such a scenario. What we are seeing instead is a steady erosion of quality of life for most people. The mass media does its best to obscure or distract from it, but anyone who wishes to see through this thin veil of denial can do so. And although the US is unlikely to achieve the same high level of collapse-preparedness as a whole, individuals and small groups within it can take a variety of steps to close the collapse gap, setting themselves up to suffer through circumstances only somewhat more dismal than those that confronted the citizens of the former Soviet Union.

Collapse Mitigation

DIRE CIRCUMSTANCES provide the impetus to Do Something. For example, the need to do something about 9/11 gave us the quagmires in Afghanistan (where the size of the opium harvest is about the only thing left to brag about) and Iraq (where there are no such bright spots). How the imperative to Do Something operates in the absence of any workable ideas will be discussed later on, under Boondoggles. For now, let the focus be on the subject of this action — the first person plural personal pronoun "we" — for it is inevitably We who are exhorted to Do Something, not "they," nor "you," nor members of the target constituency — those about whom Something Must Be Done. Normally, they are considered part of the problem, not part of the solution.

Somewhat counterintuitively, then, the scope of the problem generally determines the scope of the pronoun "we." If the problem is local, such as the prevalence of drug trafficking and prostitution on a certain street corner, the target constituency includes the easily identifiable but politically voiceless junkies, pimps and whores, and We — the activist part of the community, in cooperation with local officials — might have some effectiveness in relocating these undesirable activities to a less fashionable street corner. If the problem is global ozone depletion, then We are the fairly small community of chemical manufacturers that produce refrigerants and other CFCs, together with the governments that regulate them, making the Montreal Protocol that phased out CFCs a matter of navigating international bureaucracy. But most other problems are not so easy. When it comes to greenhouse gas emissions, the target constituency ranges from the owner of a luxury mega-yacht that burns a dozen gallons to the mile, to the equally conscientious decaying moss in the thawing tundra, and We, the sensitive environmentalist moviegoers, are unlikely to persuade either of them to change their global-warming ways.

The biggest problem facing the earth is human overpopulation, and here the target constituency is people who want to have children, who are politically unassailable. They do not even have to speak out in favor of further overpopulation. All they have to do is continue having babies, and We, the grown-up babies, can barely bring ourselves to mention the problem, never mind do anything about it. A related problem is the wave of extinction sweeping the earth due to habitat destruction: the planet is being carved up to accommodate more babies. Here, it is a popularity contest between human babies and animals, many of which are unpersonable, nameless invertebrates. These countless endangered species can never parallel the political force of the goo-goos and poops of a single human infant, although the cutest and furriest ones might be granted a new life as the infant's plush toys. This planet-devouring homunculus is now a force of nature, a weedy, invasive species going through its natural cycle of overshoot and die-off, and We who must Do Something about it are really just its gonads going through their involuntary spasms.

Whenever we confront a problem for which no political solution exists, the inevitable result is an uncomfortable impasse filled with awkward, self-censored chatter. During the Soviet establishment's fast slide toward dissolution, Gorbachev's *glasnost* campaign unleashed a torrent of words. In a sort of nation-wide talking cure, many previously taboo subjects could be broached in public, and many important problems could suddenly be discussed. An important caveat still applied: the problems always had to be cast as "specific difficulties," or "singular problems" and never as a small piece within the larger mosaic of obvious system-wide failure. The spell was really only broken by Yeltsin, when, in the aftermath of the failed *putsch,* he forcefully affixed the prefix "former" to the term "Soviet Union." At that point, old, pro-Soviet, now irrelevant standards of patriotic thought and behavior suddenly became ridiculous — the domain of half-crazed, destitute pensioners, parading with portraits of Lenin and Stalin. By then, fear of political reprisals had already faded into history, but old habits die hard, and it took years for people's thinking to catch up with the new, post-imperial reality. It was not an easy transition, and many remained embittered for life.

In today's America, it is also quite possible to talk about separate difficulties and singular problems, provided they are kept separate and singular and served up under a patriotic sauce with a dash of optimism on top. It is quite possible to refer to depressed areas, to the growing underclass and even to human rights abuses. It is, however, not allowable to refer to America as a chronically depressed country, an increasingly lower-class and impoverished country or a country that fails to take care of its citizens and often abuses them. Yes, there are prisons where heroin addicts are strapped to a chair while they go through withdrawal, a treatment so effective that some of them have to be carried out in body bags later, but that, you see, is a specific difficulty, a singular problem, if you will. But, no no no, we are a decent, freedom-loving nation in spite of such little problems. We just have a slight problem with the way we all treat each other ... and others. We did recently invade a country that had posed no threat to us and caused about a half a million civilian deaths there, but no no no, we are a peace-loving country! That is just a specific difficulty with our foreign policy, not a true reflection of our national character (which is to squirm when presented with unpleasant facts and to roll our eyes when someone draws general conclusions from them based on a preponderance of evidence).

When it comes to collapse mitigation, there is no one who will undertake an organized effort to make the collapse survivable, to save what can be saved and to avert the catastrophes that can still be averted. We will all do our best to delay or avert the collapse, possibly bringing it on sooner and making it worse. Constitutionally incapable of conceiving of a future that does not include the system that sustains our public personae, we will prattle on about a bright future for the country for as long as there is enough electricity to power the video camera that is pointed at us. Gorbachev's *perestroika* is an example of just such an effort at self-delusion: he gave speeches that ran to several hours, devoted to mystical entities such as the "socialist marketplace." He only paused to drink water — copious amounts of it, it seemed — causing people to wonder whether there was a secret chamber pot hidden inside his podium.

There are few grounds for optimism when it comes to organizing a timely and successful effort at collapse mitigation. Nevertheless, miracles do happen. For instance, in spite of inadequate preparation, in the aftermath of the Soviet collapse, none of the high-grade nuclear fissile material has ended up in the hands of terrorists, and although there were a few reports of radiation leaks, nothing happened that approached the scale of the Chernobyl catastrophe. In other ways, the miserable experience had by all was mitigated by the very nature of the Soviet system, as I described in Chapter 3. No such automatic windfalls are due the United States; here, collapse preparation, if any, is likely to be the result of an overdue, haphazard and hasty effort to provide emergency relief, organized by officials who will never admit that the state of emergency is now permanent.

The Collapse Party Platform

If the entire country were to embrace the notion that collapse is inevitable and that it must prepare for it, a new political party might be formed: the Collapse Party. If this party were to succeed in upending the two-party monopoly and form a majority government, this government would then want to implement a crash program to dismantle institutions that have no future, create new ones that are designed to survive collapse and save whatever can be saved. If, further, this crash program somehow succeeded, in spite of constitutional limitations on government action, and in spite of the inevitable lack of financial resources for such an ambitious undertaking, and in spite of the insurmountable bureaucratic complexity, then I for one would be really surprised!

Barring such surprises, it sometimes happens that events spontaneously move us in a desirable direction while governments continue to usher us along toward an unbearably grim but mercifully unlikely future. And so here are some things that I would like to spontaneously happen, in preparation for collapse.

I am particularly concerned about all the radioactive and toxic installations, stockpiles and dumps. Future generations are unlikely to be able to control them, especially if global warming puts them underwater. There is enough of this muck sitting around to kill off all of us several times over. There are abandoned mine sites at which, soon after the bulldozers and the excavators stop running, toxic tailings and the contents of settling ponds will flow into and poison the waters of major rivers, making their flood plains and estuaries uninhabitable for many centuries. Many nuclear power plants have been built near coastlines, for access to ocean water for cooling. These will be at risk of inundation due to extreme weather events and rising sea levels caused by global warming. At many nuclear power stations, spent fuel rods are stored in a pool right at the reactor site, because the search for a more permanent storage place has been mired in politics. There are surely better places to store them than next to population centers and bodies of water. Nuclear reservations — sites that have been permanently contaminated in the process of manufacturing nuclear weapons — should be marked with sufficiently large, durable and frightening obelisks to warn off travelers long after all memory of their builders has faded away.

I am also worried about soldiers getting stranded overseas — abandoning its soldiers is among the most shameful things a country can do. Not only is it an indelible stain on the country's honor, it is an effective way to create a large underclass of desperate armed men who do not answer to any authority, creating a society where the price of a contract killing is only slightly higher than the price of the ammunition. The United States maintains over a thousand overseas military bases, most of which serve no purpose other than maintaining a megalomaniac fiction of American military superiority. These are often resupplied by private contractors, whose procurement operations rely on the domestic civilian economy. As long as the economy is intact, they can bring three flavors of ice cream to an air-conditioned tent in the middle of a desert, but once the economy collapses, they will collapse with it, and the military may turn out to lack even the resources to truck in water. Overseas military bases should be dismantled and the troops repatriated.

I would like to see the huge prison population whittled away in a controlled manner, ahead of time, instead of in a chaotic general amnesty. Such an amnesty will have to happen as a matter of course, once the resources that sustain the prison system stop flowing. The scenario to avoid is one in which, in the midst of general chaos, the entire population of prisoners is released en masse and, with no other resources available to them, they start plying their various criminal trades. Paroling the non-violent, shortening sentences, decriminalizing drugs and providing room and board to former inmates are all reasonable steps to take to prevent a crime wave of staggering proportions once the criminal justice system finally shuts down.

Lastly, I think that this farce with debts that will never be repaid has gone on long enough. Collateralized debt will evaporate once the value of the collateral is too low to secure the debt: if the house has no water and cannot be illuminated, heated or reached by transportation, its value is effectively zero, and so is the value of the mortgage. In fact, its value should properly be regarded as negative, since it will cost money to knock it down and reclaim the land. In the post-bankruptcy-reform era, non-collateralized debt, such as student loans or credit card debt, is secured by the threat of force — be it breaking legs or garnering wages — and even such measures bring diminishing returns in a collapsing economy. Wiping the slate clean ahead of time will give society some time to readjust to the new reality. Perhaps most importantly, by canceling debts before they become unrepayable, it may be possible to prevent the current system — one of indentured servitude based on debt — from evolving into a system of permanent servitude based on force: a new American slavery. I remain optimistic that the forces of chaos will prevent such a system from becoming entrenched; nevertheless, it might be prudent to take some measures to make such an outcome even less likely.

❀ ❀ ❀

It has been two years since I wrote this platform for the Collapse Party, and I am happy to report that, without recruiting any members or fielding any candidates, the party has made significant progress toward implementing its agenda.

Of course it would be too much to ask that the US government shut down its nuclear industry, dismantle nuclear installations and sequester radioactive materials in geologically stable places. But we at Collapse Party headquarters are happy to report that not a single new nuclear power plant has been commissioned in the past two years, and although there are still some projects winding their way through the tortuous planning process, we remain confident that none of them will ever be built. While the nuclear problem has not gone away, nor has it grown appreciably worse.

Although the US military remains just as ruinously expensive and incapable of victory as it was two years ago, troops are being pulled out of Iraq in what amounts to a clear admission of defeat. This is made plain by the fact that the Iraqis are unwilling to even form a national government, knowing full well that their country is now defunct and will lapse into civil war as soon as the Americans are finally driven out. Next in line is Afghanistan, where NATO is gearing up to hand control back to the Taliban, at which point please make sure that President Hamid Karzai's mail goes straight to Dubai, because I doubt that the Taliban will bother forwarding it. Meanwhile the defense budget is being cut, and then cut some more, defense contractors are scaling back and laying off senior staff, and before long America's military "lily pads" around the world will succumb to a domino effect. The nagging question is what to do with repatriated troops, since there are no civilian jobs for them. The Collapse Party proposal is to organize them into units to provide neighborhood-level security, poised to take over just as problems with municipal budgets cause the police to fade from the scene.

Although US jails continue to incarcerate the largest percentage of the population of any country on earth, we at the Collapse Party are heartened by the fact that the American Gulag has finally stopped growing. The dire fiscal condition of many states is forcing them to parole tens of thousands of prisoners. But instead of providing them with free room and board upon release, as we have repeatedly urged, the officials wait for them to commit a crime and then lock them up again. This practice is, needless to say, not only inefficient from a fiscal point of view, but poses a threat to public health. We urge officials everywhere to put a stop to this wasteful "release and catch" behavior and to seek more cost-effective approaches.

Although the US government is as far as ever from considering instituting a Biblical jubilee (forgiveness of all debts, public and private), there are some glimmers of hope here as well. Many people have discovered that nothing particularly bad happens when they walk away from a mortgage that has become onerous. More people are discovering that nobody in particular owns their mortgage because the chain of title was broken in the act of slicing and packaging it for sale as part of a Collateralized Debt Obligation (aka "toxic asset," of the sort that now litters the vaults at the Federal Reserve). These assets are not just toxic — they are not even legal, and so the mortgage cannot be foreclosed upon. Still other debtors are becoming proficient at suing collection companies — a fun and lucrative sport. All that is required to lay the trap is knowledge of a few obscure laws, a tape recorder, some legal forms, and the ability to answer the telephone in a feigned tone of utter helplessness. Slaying the hydra of the US debt racket takes a lot of doing: bludgeon it, stab it, drown it, set it on fire ... every bit helps, but for heaven's sake don't feed it!

Political Solutions

Before, during and immediately after the Soviet collapse, there was a great deal of political activity by groups we might regard as progressive: liberal, environmentalist, pro-democracy reformers. These grew out of the dissident movements of the Soviet era and made quite a significant impact for a time. A decade later "democracy" and "liberalism" are generally considered dirty words in Russia, commonly associated with exploitation of Russia by foreigners and other rot. The Russian state is centrist, with authoritarian tendencies. Most Russians dislike and distrust their government but are afraid of weakness, and want a strong hand at the helm.

It is easy to see why political idealism fails to thrive in the murky post-collapse political environment. There is a strong pull to the right by nationalists who want to find scapegoats (inevitably, foreigners and ethnic minorities), a strong pull to the center by members of the ancien régime trying to hold on to remnants of their power, and a great upwelling of indecision, confusion and inconclusive debate on the left by those trying to do good and failing to do anything. Sometimes the liberals get a chance to try an experiment or two. Yegor Gaidar got to try some liberal economic reforms as the prime minister in the post-Soviet government of Boris Yeltsin. He was a tragicomic figure, and many Russians now cringe when remembering his efforts (and to be fair, we don't even know how helpful or damaging his reforms might have been, since most of them were never implemented). Upon his death last year a debate broke out in Russia between those who maintained that his actions were those of an incompetent and those who maintained that nobody would have known what to do given the horrific economic conditions of that period. He simply tried various things, day to day, hoping that one of them would restart the economy. If he were still alive, he might feel quite at home on the US Council of Economic Advisors: they don't know how to restart the economy either.

Liberals, reformers and progressives in the United States, whether self-styled or so labeled, have had a hard time implementing their agenda. Even their few hard-won victories, such as Social Security, may get dismantled. Even when they managed to elect a president more to their liking, the effects were, by Western standards, reactionary. There was the Carter doctrine, according to which the United States will protect its access to oil by military aggression if necessary. There was also Clinton's welfare reform, which forced single mothers to work menial jobs while placing their children in substandard daycare.

People in the United States and the Soviet Union have broadly similar attitudes toward politics. In the US, this is often referred to as "voter apathy," but it might be more accurately described as nonvoter indifference. The Soviet Union had a single, entrenched, systemically corrupt political party, which held a monopoly on power. The US has two entrenched, systemically corrupt political parties, whose positions are often indistinguishable and which together hold a monopoly on power. In either case, there is, or was, a single governing elite, but in the United States it organized itself into opposing teams to make its stranglehold on power seem more sportsmanlike.

In the US, there is an industry of political commentators and pundits that is devoted to inflaming political passions as much as possible, especially before elections. This is similar to what sports writers and commentators do to draw attention to their game. It seems that the main force behind political discourse in the US is boredom: one can chat about the weather, one's job, one's mortgage and how it relates to current and projected property values, cars and the traffic situation, sports and, far behind sports, politics. In an effort to make people pay attention, most of the issues trotted out before the electorate pertain to reproduction: abortion, birth control, stem cell research and similar small bits of social policy are bandied about rather than settled, simply because they get good ratings. "Boring" but vitally important strategic issues such as sustainable development, environmental protection and energy policy are studiously avoided.

Although people often bemoan political apathy as if it were a grave social ill, it seems to me that this is just as it should be. Why should essentially powerless people want to engage in a humiliating farce designed to demonstrate the legitimacy of those who wield the power? In Soviet-era Russia, intelligent people did their best to ignore the Communists: paying attention to them, whether through criticism or praise, would only serve to give them comfort and encouragement, making them feel as if they mattered. Why should Americans want to act any differently with regard to the Republicans and the Democrats? For love of donkeys and elephants?

Private Sector Solutions

Certain Soviet state enterprises were basically states within states. They controlled what amounted to an entire economic system and could go on even without the larger economy. They kept to this arrangement even after they were privatized. They drove Western management consultants mad with their endless kindergartens, retirement homes, laundries, clinics and vacation resorts. These weren't part of their core competency, you see. They needed to divest and streamline their operations. The Western management gurus overlooked the most important thing: the core competency of these enterprises lay in their ability to survive economic collapse. Maybe the young geniuses at Google can wrap their heads around this one, but I doubt that their stockholders will.

To make itself collapse-proof, a company would need to follow a strategy that is antithetical to how a business is supposed to operate. It would have to consciously eliminate suppliers, cancel outsourcing arrangements and move all production and operations in-house. It would then need to shrug off investors, taking the company private if it is public, thus eliminating the need to generate a profit. Lastly it would need to eliminate the need for customers and for cash flow, adapting the mode of only serving its own employees. Within the context of a collapsing economy, this would require the company to diversify its operation, to include mining, manufacturing, farming, transportation, housing (including retirement homes), health care, education, security and entertainment — to provide everything that its work force might require. Provided all of the previous steps were carried out successfully, the company could then cut the work week down to a nominal few hours, provide month-long vacations, and lower the retirement age to the mid-50s: a worker's paradise on earth.

There do not appear to exist any commercial entities in the United States that would be capable of following such a plan. The bigger entities that own a sufficient range of facilities, be they public, semi-public or private — the armed forces, for instance, or the larger universities — are far too addicted to both public and private money, and have outsourced too many functions to be able to draw them in-house in time.

But an even bigger hurdle is psychological: there is nothing to force the required radical shift in thinking. In the Soviet Union it occurred gradually, over generations, as the industrial behemoths begot by central planning adjusted to the shortcomings of the same central planning system by drawing in as many support functions as they could. There is no mechanism by which Americans can reproduce any of the proverbial Soviet industrial conglomerates such as Uralmash or Gazprom quickly. Moreover, there is no longer even the domestic industrial base to support industrial operations on such a massive scale: a lot of the equipment and stock would have to be imported, negating the premise. Thus, while successful private sector solutions to collapse mitigation might not be impossible, they are very, very unlikely.

Activism and Apathy

Crisis-mitigating agendas for "us" to implement, whether they involve wars over access to resources, nuclear plant construction, wind farms or hydrogen dreams, are not likely to be implemented, because this "we" entity will no longer be functional. If we are not likely to be able to implement our agenda prior to the collapse, then whatever is left of us is even less likely to do so afterward. Thus, there is little reason to organize politically in order to try to do good. But if you want to prepare to take advantage of a bad situation — well, that's a different story!

Politics has great potential for making a bad situation worse. It can cause war, ethnic cleansing and genocide. Whenever people gather into political organizations, whether voluntarily or forcibly, it is a sign of trouble. I was at the annual meeting of my community garden recently and among the generally placid and shy group of gardeners there were a couple of self-styled "activists." Before too long, one of these was raising the question of expelling people. People who don't show up for annual meetings and don't sign up to do cleaning and composting and so on — why are they allowed to hold on to their plots? Well, some of the "rogue elements" the activist was referring to consisted of elderly Russians who, due to their extensive experience with such things during the Soviet times, are exceedingly unlikely to ever be compelled to take part in communal labor or sit through meetings with the collective. Frankly, they would prefer death. But they also love to garden.

The reason the "element" is allowed to exist in this particular community garden is because the woman who runs the place allows them to hold on to their plots. It is her decision: she exercises leadership and she does not engage in politics. She makes the garden function, and allows the activists to make their noise, once a year, with no ill effects. But if the situation were to change and the kitchen garden suddenly became a source of sustenance rather than a hobby, how long would it take before the activist element would start demanding more power and asserting its authority?

Leadership is certainly a helpful quality in a crisis, which is a particularly bad time for lengthy deliberations and debates. In any situation, some people are better equipped to handle it than others, and can help others by giving them directions. They naturally accumulate a certain amount of power for themselves, and this is fine as long as enough people benefit from it, and as long as nobody is harmed or oppressed. Such people often spontaneously emerge in a crisis.

An equally useful quality in a crisis is apathy. The Russian people are exceptionally patient: even in the worst of post-collapse times, they did not riot and there were no significant protests. They coped as best they could. The safest group of people to be with in a crisis is one that does not share strong ideological convictions, is not easily swayed by argument and does not possess an overdeveloped, exclusive sense of identity.

Clueless busybodies who feel that they must Do Something and can be spun around by any half-wit demagogue are bad enough, but the most dangerous group, and one to watch out for and run from, is a group of political activists resolved to organize and promote some program or other. Even if the program is benign, even if it is beneficial, the politicized approach to solving it might not be either. As the saying goes, revolutions eat their children. Then they turn on everyone else. The life of a refugee is a form of survival; staying and fighting an organized mob generally is not.

Boondoggles to the Rescue!

Economic collapse has a way of turning economic negatives into positives. It is not necessary for the United States to embrace the tenets of command economy and central planning to match the Soviet lackluster performance in this area. We have our own methods that are working almost as well. I call them "boondoggles." They are solutions to problems that result in more severe problems than those they attempt to solve.

Just look around and you will see boondoggles sprouting up everywhere, in every field of endeavor: we have military boondoggles like Iraq, financial boondoggles like the doomed retirement system, medical boondoggles like private health insurance and legal boondoggles like the intellectual property system. At some point, creating another boondoggle becomes the preferred course of action: since the outcome can be predicted with complete accuracy, there is little risk. Proposing a solution that might work runs the risk of it not working.

So why not, as a matter of policy, only propose solutions that are guaranteed to simply create more problems, for which further solutions can then be proposed? At some point, a boondoggle event horizon is reached, like the light event horizon that exists at the surface of a black hole. Beyond that horizon, the only possible course of action is to create more boondoggles.

The combined weight of all these boondoggles is slowly but surely pushing us all down. If it pushes us down far enough, then economic collapse, when it arrives, will be like falling out of a ground-floor window. We just have to help this process along, or at least not interfere with it. So if somebody comes to you and says, "I want to make a boondoggle that runs on hydrogen" — by all means encourage him! It's not as good as a boondoggle that burns money directly, but it's a step in the right direction.

Once you understand the principles involved, boondoggling will come naturally. Let us work through a sample problem: there is no longer enough gasoline to go around. A simple but effective solution is to ban the sale of new cars, with the exception of certain fleet vehicles used by public services. First, older cars are overall more energy-efficient than new cars, because the massive amount of energy that went into manufacturing them is more highly amortized. Second, large energy savings accrue from the shutdown of an entire industry devoted to designing, building, marketing and financing new cars. Third, older cars require more maintenance, reinvigorating the local economy at the expense of mainly foreign car manufacturers, and helping reduce the trade deficit. Fourth, this will create a shortage of cars, translating automatically into fewer, shorter car trips, a higher passenger occupancy per trip and more bicycling and use of public transportation, saving even more energy. Lastly, this would allow the car to be made obsolete on about the same time line as the oil industry that made it possible.

Of course, this solution does not qualify as a boondoggle, so it will not be seriously considered. The problems it creates are too small, and they offer too little scope for creating further boondoggles. Moreover, if this solution worked, then everyone would be happily driving their slightly older cars, completely unprepared for some inevitable, cataclysmic, economy-collapsing event. It is better to introduce some boondoggles, such as corn-based ethanol and coal-to-liquids conversion. Ethanol production creates very little additional energy but it does create some fantastic problems for further boondoggling: a shortage of food and higher food prices, malnutrition among the poor and inflation. It also reinforces a large existing boondoggle: by funneling resources to petrochemical-based agribusiness, which depletes and poisons the soil and has no future in an age when petrochemicals are scarce, it helps undermine future food security.

Coal-to-liquids conversion offers similarly excellent opportunities. By attempting to alleviate a shortage of gasoline, it will cause a shortage of coal, resulting in power outages and dramatically higher electricity rates. It will add more carbon dioxide to the atmosphere, accelerating global warming. It will probably call for some coal imports, inefficiently moving a very bulky fuel from far away, and fostering energy dependence on suppliers such as China and Russia, further enhancing the trade deficit. Along with corn-based ethanol, this excellent boondoggle reinforces the erroneous notion that Americans will be able to continue to drive cars into the indefinite future, conditioning them to clamor for more boondoggles in place of any real solutions.

With a bit of practice, you should be able to come up with some excellent boondoggles of your own in your own field of endeavor. If your boondoggle works, it will create more problems for you to solve in the next round, as long as there is time for one more round. And if there is not, then you will be where you want to be: at a ground-floor window, staring into an abyss of only a couple of feet. Although by then it may feel unnatural, at that point you must resist the temptation to create yet another boondoggle by jumping down headfirst.

Investment Advice

Often when people hear about the possibility of economic collapse, they wonder, "Let's suppose that the US economy is going to collapse soon. Why is this even worth thinking about, if there is nothing I can do about it?" Well, I am not a professional investment advisor, so I risk nothing by making some suggestions for how one can collapse-proof one's investment portfolio.

The nuclear scare gave rise to the archetype of the American Survivalist, holed up in the hills with a bomb shelter, a fantastic number of tins of Spam and an assortment of guns and plentiful ammunition with which to fight off neighbors from further downhill, or perhaps just to shoot beer cans when the neighbors come over for beer and Spamwiches. And, of course, an American flag. This sort of survivalism is about as good as burying yourself alive, I suppose.

The idea of stockpiling is not altogether bad, though. Stockpiling food is, of course, a rotten idea, literally. But certain manufactured items are certainly worth considering. Suppose you have a retirement account, or some mutual funds. And suppose you feel reasonably certain that by the time you are scheduled to retire this won't be enough to buy a cup of coffee. And suppose you realize that you can currently buy a lot of good stuff that has a long shelf life and will be needed and valuable far into the future. And suppose, further, that you have a small amount of storage space: a few hundred square feet. Now, what are you going to do? Sit by and watch your savings evaporate? Or take the tax hit and invest in things that are not composed of vapor?

Once the cash machines are out of cash, the stock ticker stops ticking and the retail chain breaks down, people will still have basic needs. There will be flea markets and private barter arrangements to serve these needs, using whatever local token of exchange is available: bundles of hundred dollar bills, bits of gold chain, packs of cigarettes or what have you. It's not a bad idea to own a few of everything you will need, but you should also invest in things you will be able to trade for things you will need. Think of consumer necessities that require high technology and have a long shelf life. Here are some suggestions to get you started: drugs (over-the-counter and prescription), razor blades, condoms. Toiletries, such as good soap, will be luxury items. Fill some shipping containers, nitrogen-pack them so that nothing rusts or rots and store them somewhere.

After the Soviet collapse, there swiftly appeared a category of itinerant merchants who provided people with access to imported products. To procure their wares, these people had to travel abroad, to Poland, to China, to Turkey, on trains, carrying goods back and forth in their baggage. They would exchange a suitcase of Russian-made watches for a suitcase of other, more useful consumer products, such as shampoo or razor blades. They would have to grease the palms of officials along their route, and were often robbed. There was a period of time when these people, called *chelnoki*, which is Russian for "shuttles," were the only source of consumer products. The products were often factory rejects, damaged or past their sell-by date, but this did not make them any less valuable. Based on their example, it is possible to predict which items will be in high demand and to stockpile these items ahead of time, as a hedge against economic collapse. Note that *chelnoki* had intact economies to trade with, accessible by train — this is not guaranteed to be the case in the US.

A stockpile of this sort, in a walkable, socially stable place, where you know everybody, where you have some close friends and some family, where you own your shelter and some land free and clear, and where you can grow most of your own food and barter for the rest, should enable you to survive economic collapse without too much trouble. And, who knows, maybe you will even find happiness there.

The Future is Rated "B"

My voluminous fan mail has made me aware of a curious fact: many of my readers seem persuaded that the future is either *Mad Max* or *Waterworld*. As far as they are concerned, there just aren't any other options. What's more, some people have even tried to venture a guess as to which of the two it shall be by watching what I do. I live on a boat, and that is apparently an indication that the future must be *Waterworld*–like. But I have also been seen rattling around town on a rusty old motorcycle, and that is taken as an indication of a more *Mad Max*–like future.

It saddens me that so few people bring up the film *Blade Runner*, and it is even more sad that George Lucas's *THX 1138* or Jean-Luc Godard's *Alphaville* are almost never mentioned, because these particular films have in many ways proven to be predictive of the present rather than just the future. Take *THX 1138*, for example: it is about some people who live in a sealed-off, climate-controlled environment, are on a compulsory regimen of psychoactive drugs, are assigned their mates by a computer program, and watch pornography that is piped into their living rooms in order to relax after work. When they refuse to take their meds, they are abused by robot-like police armed with electric cattle prods. When one of them escapes into the wilderness, it turns out that the police lack the budget to hunt him down. That may have seemed a bit exotic and futuristic back in 1971 when Lucas filmed it, but now describes the people who live down the street. *Alphaville*, on the other hand, is vaguely reminiscent of some of my more interesting business trips.

People seem uncomfortable with the idea that works of fiction can predict the present, because the present is supposed to be reality, not fiction. The future, on the other hand, is fair game, because it is supposed to be purely fictional: it is common wisdom, you see, that the future is unknowable. Thus artists are free to paint the future any color they like, while the more scientifically minded approach it by formulating alternative scenarios. It is useless to try to tell them that there is just the one scenario, apparently written by some incompetent hack, and that, even though it stinks, it is high time they stopped flapping their gums about alternative ones and started auditioning for a role in this one, since it happens to be the only one that is actually being produced.

For the benefit of those who believe that the future is fictional but the present is real, it may be helpful to point out that the present is largely fictional as well. Here's a perfectly good example: do you remember those valiant freedom fighters who expelled foreign invaders from their ancient land — the mujahideen? What do you think happened to them? Well, they've been re-branded as the Taliban, and are now evil. Same Pashtun tribesmen (or their sons) toting the same AK–47s and carrying out the same missions against strangely similar infidel invaders have, by the simple act of renaming, been transformed from valiant warriors into cowardly fiends.

The people whose job it is to write the fiction that we are expected to accept as our one real and true present don't seem to have much of an imagination. They also seem to have a rather short reading list and lift their ideas from just a handful of slender volumes. George Orwell's *1984* and Aldous Huxley's *Brave New World* are their particular favorites, along with Franz Kafka's *The Trial*. Take, for instance, the cult of Osama bin Laden as the mastermind of the 9/11 attacks: it is an image of the perpetual enemy lifted straight out of Orwell. We may quite reasonably suppose that Osama was a sickly CIA operative who succumbed to renal failure a long time ago and was posthumously demonized using some grainy amateur videos and a few muffled audio tapes featuring another CIA operative whose code name is "Elvis." For years now Osama's restless and lonely ghost, clad in white robes and towing a broken dialysis machine across the rugged and bare mountain passes of Waziristan, has been relentlessly hunted by a swarm of endlessly circling Predator drones. The war in Afghanistan is currently costing the USA $300 million a day. Sorry to bring up yet another B movie, but how much did "Ghostbusters" charge per visit?

I have no wish to debate these topics, and would urge you to shy away from them as well. There are just a few people who know enough about them, and they generally have no wish to debate them either. There is nothing in it for them — or anyone else. Just about everyone else is either wallowing in blissful ignorance or has been subjected to a mind control process used in advertising: proof through repetition. Here is a contemporary example: a purely fictional phenomenon from the 9/11 season of 2010 known as "The mosque at Ground Zero." The kernel of truth behind this mainly fictional story is the proposed Islamic cultural center, not a mosque, to be built at a location that is nowhere near Ground Zero, but we now live in a realm of compulsory fiction, reinforced through repetition in the echo chamber of the media, which makes truth irrelevant. Once the media start ranting and raving like that, it is hard for them to stop, and next they trot out some obscure evangelical pastor from Florida who wants to burn a stack of Korans, and they cannot for the life of them stop talking about him either. When in response violent demonstrations erupt in already violent places that are patrolled by US soldiers, that just adds spice to this already wonderful story. I hope that you are beginning to see a pattern here: first a country goes a little bit senile, then noticeably demented, then completely stark, raving, running-about-naked-smearing-feces-all-over-itself insane. Then it hurts itself. Individual insanity is rare, but group insanity is, unfortunately, the bane of societies that are nearing their end.

It would seem that, if you are a certain kind of popular author, a good way to ensure that the future comes to resemble your worst nightmares is to write a novel about them. This has certainly worked for Orwell, Huxley and Kafka. But there is also an alternative: compose your own fiction instead of accepting anyone else's, then go ahead and turn it into reality. A good first step might be to write a short story. It can be very short, and it doesn't even have to be particularly interesting. Something as trivial as this might do for starters: "The next morning she woke up and, instead of having a bagel with cream cheese and a cup of coffee for breakfast, she fasted until sundown." And then, the next morning, she woke up, and something curious happened: this short story came to life, and so it came to pass. Next came other stories, each a bit longer than the previous one, bridging the present and the future in new ways, and eventually spanning decades. And as these decades rolled by, these stories too came to life.

This, as I see it, is the best way forward in a depressed and increasingly demented and accident-prone country that is heading straight for collapse, where the present (reality, what people think is going on, common notions of the state of things) is degenerating into useless noise — the clamor of clueless but self-important people desperately begging you to continue giving them your attention, so that they can stuff your head with more B-rated trash. But if you ignore them long enough, they will go away. Don't hope, don't wish, don't dream, but do write your own fiction and use it to create a present that works for you. Invent places for yourself and for those you care about in your stories about the future, and then go ahead and live in them. You don't have to settle for anyone else's B-rated nonsense. And don't let anyone tell you that you are crazy or living in a dream. It's not a dream, dammit, it's a work of fiction!

Starve the Beast

Many types of mainstream economic behavior are not prudent on a personal level and are also counterproductive when trying to invent a personal strategy for mitigating collapse. Any behavior that might supposedly result in continued economic growth and prosperity should be regarded as immediately suspicious and probably counterproductive: the higher you jump, the harder you land. It is traumatic to go from having a big retirement fund to having no retirement fund because of a market crash. It is also traumatic to go from a high income to little or no income. If, on top of that, you have kept yourself incredibly busy and suddenly have nothing to do, then you will really be in rough shape.

Economic collapse is about the worst possible time for someone to suffer a nervous breakdown, yet this is what often happens. The people who are most at risk psychologically are successful middle-aged men. When their career is suddenly over, their savings gone and their property worthless, much of their sense of self-worth goes as well. They tend to drink themselves to death and commit suicide in disproportionate numbers. Since they also tend to be the most experienced and capable people, this is a staggering loss to society. They would be well advised to cash out early and spend time learning how to redefine personal success in ways that are not critically dependent on their continued ability to produce and consume.

If the economy, and your place within it, are really important to you, you will be really hurt when they go away. You can cultivate an attitude of studied indifference, but it has to be more than just a conceit. You have to develop the lifestyle, habits and physical stamina to back it up. Those who have been brought up to compete against others tend to take it particularly hard when faced with widespread failure, because they have lost the ability to pity anyone — least of all themselves. The trick is to embrace failure — yours and everyone else's

— without allowing it to embrace you. Needless to say, if you can't manage this, you won't be much of a success moving forward.

It takes a lot of creativity and effort to put together a fulfilling existence on the margins of society. At first it will take a lot out of you to eat humble pie and pretend that it is delicious. You might find yourself among some sketchy, marginal people, and suddenly realize that they are nicer to each other and, incidentally, to you, than your very own permanently dissatisfied ilk. These might be marginal people leading marginal existences on the margins of society. But after the collapse, you may just discover that these margins are some of the best places to live.

Adaptation

SOMETIMES, THE SOCIALLY PROACTIVE approach seems to be rather a waste of time. Rather than attempting to undertake the Herculean task of mitigating the unmitigatable — attempting to stop the world and point it in a different direction — it seems far better to turn inward and work to transform yourself into someone who might stand a chance, given the world's assumed trajectory. Much of this transformation is psychological and involves letting go of many notions that we have been conditioned to accept unquestioningly. Some of it involves acquiring new skills and a different set of habits. Some of it is even physiological, changing one's body to prepare it for a life that has far fewer creature comforts and conveniences, while requiring far more physical labor.

It must be understood that not everyone is able to adapt. There are many who are, even to their own mind, a sum total of their character flaws: take away their bad habits and what would be left of them except some nameless fear? Many others, though they may be convinced that certain unpleasant changes are necessary, are unwilling to endure any unnecessary inconveniences or discomforts until circumstances force them to do so, and ipso facto will choose to remain unprepared. Finally, there are plenty of those who, whether by choice or by accident, have so encumbered themselves by their current living arrangement that they have left themselves no means of escape and no opportunity for making gradual changes. These, and many others, are likely to have a most unpleasant experience when brought face to face with catastrophe.

But if you do have a modicum of freedom and the ability to change course, consider the following two points. First, you are that strangest inhabitant of the animal kingdom — an animal that can evolve without undergoing genetic mutation. You can evolve culturally. And since cultural mutations are never random, your evolution can be fast. Second, you need not inform any other living thing of your new status as a cultural mutant. To all outward appearances, you can remain indistinguishable from the rest of the herd. But the space and time in which you move will no longer be the space and time created and allotted by society, but those that you have carved out for yourself by reducing your needs, expanding your abilities and shedding the habits, both mental and physical, by which others are enslaved.

In order to adapt, you will need plenty of free time. Granting yourself this time requires a leap of faith: you have to assume that the future has already arrived. Your lying eyes will be of little help here, so shut them tight. The old normal is that life will go on just like before. The new normal is that nothing will ever be the same. Your consolation is that even if the new normal never arrives, you will be well adapted for that, too.

Loss of "Normalcy"

An early victim of collapse is the sense of normalcy. People are initially shocked to find that it's missing, but quickly forget that such a thing ever existed, except for the odd vague twinge of nostalgia. Normalcy is never exactly normal: in an industrial economy, the sense of normalcy is an artificial, manufactured item.

We may be hurtling towards environmental doom and, thankfully, never quite get there because of resource depletion, but, in the meantime, the lights are on, there is traffic on the streets and, even if the lights go out for a while due to a blackout, they will be back on in due course and the shops will reopen. Business as usual will resume. The sumptuous buffet lunch will be served on time, so that the assembled luminaries can resume discussion of measured steps we all need to take to avert certain disaster. But the lunch is not served; then the lights go out. At some point, somebody calls the whole thing a farce, and the luminaries adjourn forever.

In Russia, normalcy broke down in a series of steps. First, people stopped being afraid to speak their mind. Then they stopped taking the authorities seriously. Lastly, the authorities stopped taking each other seriously. In the final act, Yeltsin stood on top of a Red Army tank with the Russian tricolor flag for a backdrop and spoke the words, "Former Soviet Union."

In the Soviet Union, as this thing called normalcy wore thin due to the stalemate in Afghanistan, the Chernobyl disaster and general economic stagnation, it continued to be enforced through careful management of the mass media well into the period known as *perestroika*. In the United States, as the economy fails to create enough jobs for several years in a row and the entire country tilts towards bankruptcy, business as usual continues to be a top-selling product, or so we are led to believe. American normalcy circa 2005 seemed as impregnable as Soviet normalcy circa 1985.

If there is a difference between the Soviet and American approaches to maintaining a sense of normalcy, it is this: the Soviets tried to maintain it by force, while the Americans' superior approach is to maintain theirs through fear. You tend to feel more normal if you fear falling off your perch and cling to it for dear life than if somebody nails your feet to it.

More to the point: in a consumer society, anything that puts people off their shopping is dangerously disruptive, and all consumers sense this. Any expression of the truth about our lack of prospects for continued existence as a highly developed, prosperous industrial society is disruptive to the consumerist collective unconscious. There is a herd instinct to reject it, and therefore it fails, not through any overt action, but by failing to turn a profit because it is unpopular.

In spite of this small difference in how normalcy is or was enforced, it was brought down, in the late Soviet Union as in the contemporary United States, through almost identical means, although with different technology. In the Soviet Union, there was something called *samizdat*, or self-publishing: with the help of manual typewriters and carbon paper, Russian dissidents managed to circulate enough material to neutralize the effects of enforced normalcy. In the contemporary United States, we have websites and bloggers: different technology, same difference. These are writings for which enforced normalcy is no longer the norm; the norm is the truth — or at least someone's earnest approximation of it.

So what has become of these Soviet mavericks, some of whom foretold the coming collapse with reasonable accuracy? To be brief, they faded from view. Both tragically and ironically, those who become experts in explaining the faults of the system and in predicting the course of its demise are very much part of the system. When the system disappears, so does their area of expertise and their audience. People stop intellectualizing their predicament and start trying to escape it — through drink or drugs or creativity or cunning — but they have no time for pondering the larger context.

Smelling the Roses

Once the economy collapses, there is generally less to do, making it a good time for the naturally idle and a bad time for those predisposed to keeping busy. Soviet-era culture had room for two types of activity: normal, which generally meant avoiding breaking a sweat, and heroic. Normal activity was expected, and there was never any reason to do it harder than expected. In fact, that sort of thing tended to be frowned upon by "the collective," or the rank and file. Heroic activity was celebrated, but not necessarily rewarded financially.

Russians tend to look in bemused puzzlement on the American compulsion to "work hard and play hard." The term "career" was in the Soviet days a pejorative term — the attribute of a "careerist" — someone greedy, unscrupulous and overly "ambitious" (also a pejorative term). Terms like "success" and "achievement" were very rarely applied on a personal level, because they sounded overweening and pompous. They were reserved for bombastic public pronouncements about the great successes of the Soviet people. Not that positive personal characteristics did not exist: on a personal level, respect was given to talent, professionalism, decency, sometimes even creativity. But to a Russian, "hard worker" sounded a lot like "fool."

A collapsing economy is especially hard on those who are accustomed to prompt, courteous service. In the Soviet Union, most official service was rude and slow and involved standing in long lines. Many of the products that were in short supply could not be obtained even in this manner, and required something called *blat*: special, unofficial access or favor. The exchange of personal favors was far more important to the actual functioning of the economy than the exchange of money. To Russians, *blat* is almost a sacred thing: a vital part of culture that holds society together. It is also the only part of the economy that is collapse-proof, and, as such, a valuable cultural adaptation.

Most Americans have heard of communism, and automatically believe that it is an apt description of the Soviet system, even though there was nothing particularly communal about a welfare state and a vast industrial empire run by an elitist central planning bureaucracy. But very few of them have ever heard of the real operative "ism" that dominated Soviet life: *dofenism*, which can be loosely translated as "not giving a rat's ass." A lot of people, more and more during the "stagnation" period of the 1980s, felt nothing but contempt for the system, did what little they had to do to get by (night watchman and furnace stoker were favorite jobs among the highly educated) and got all their pleasure from their friends, from their reading or from nature.

This sort of disposition may seem like a cop-out, but when there is a collapse on the horizon, it works as psychological insurance: instead of going through the agonizing process of losing and rediscovering one's identity in a post-collapse environment, one could simply sit back and watch events unfold. If you are currently a "mover and shaker," of things or people or whatever, then collapse will surely come as a shock to you, and it will take you a long time, perhaps forever, to find more things to move and shake to your satisfaction. However, if your current occupation is as a keen observer of grass and trees, then post-collapse you could take on something else that's useful, such as dismantling useless things.

The ability to stop and smell the roses — to let it all go, to refuse to harbor regrets or nurture grievances, to confine one's serious attention only to that which is immediately necessary and not to worry too much about the rest — is perhaps the one, most critical attribute required for post-collapse survival. The most psychologically devastated are usually the middle-aged breadwinners who, once they are no longer gainfully employed, feel completely lost. Detachment and indifference can be most healing, provided they do not become morbid. It helps to get over your sentimental nostalgia for what once was early on.

Comforts and Necessities

Economic progress creates a ratcheting effect, by which what are at first comforts and conveniences gradually become necessities. For example, most Americans will tell you that owning a car is a necessity. But even clothing and shoes are, strictly speaking, not necessities: we evolved bipedal locomotion and ran around the planet naked and barefoot for all but the last few thousand years. Most of us still can, and some of us still enjoy doing so when we can. Most Americans will also tell you that things like indoor running water, flush toilets, central heating and on-demand hot water are necessities. In fact, they are luxuries.

True necessities are those few items found at the base of Maslow's necessity hierarchy: oxygen, water and food, in that order. The order is determined by seeing how long someone can stay alive when deprived of any of these: a few minutes for oxygen; a few days for water; a few weeks for food. These are followed by non-necessities such as shelter, companionship, opportunities for sexual release and meaningful activities such as exercise, play or work. Most people can survive without these for months, perhaps years; I even know some people who have survived for their entire lifetime without work. Cars, water heaters and flush toilets are not anywhere on this list. Sanitation is important for avoiding disease, but there are many other ways to achieve this than by diluting excrement with drinking water and flushing it down a sewer.

The problem with the luxuries that are considered necessities is that those who have come to consider them necessities, when they are suddenly deprived of them, become preoccupied by an overwhelming feeling of unwellness, making them poor company for a time. When I was in St. Petersburg in the summer of 1995, there was no running hot water in much of the city. The exceptions were a few apartments in the old parts of town, which had antique inline gas water heaters that produced a trickle of warm shower water. I was renting a room in one such apartment and people would come over to visit me, but really just to take a hot shower. The Russians did it for the luxury; the rest of the time, they showered in cold water, went to a public bath (a venerable institution, found in many countries, Russia included) or had a periodic splash in a washbasin that they filled from a kettle. The visiting Americans did it to get back to feeling normal again. Conditioned to perform a certain daily ablution, when deprived of it they itched, were offended by their own smell and had trouble holding their own around other people.

Turning the comfort-necessity dichotomy completely around, beyond the first three (air, water, food), the only true necessity for survival is discomfort. Deprived of discomfort, our bodies turn into a tender, marshmallowy mess. To shed a false necessity, it is necessary to endure discomfort for a time — sometimes months or years. To eliminate the need for shoes, you need to go barefoot and endure the pain and the blisters until calluses develop and your gait reverts to its original unshod design — although your toes, stunted and deformed by a lifetime of cruel footwear, may never regain their full dirt-gripping power. To eliminate the need for warm clothing, you need to underdress for the weather, shivering as needed until your body improves its capacity for non-shivering thermogenesis by developing layers of vascularized, brown fat that can directly generate heat. To eliminate the need for washing, you need to stop washing until the body stops constantly re-secreting the protective layer of oil that soap constantly washes away. This is best done away from other people. To eliminate the need for three meals a day, habitually exert yourself for long periods of time while fasting and only let yourself eat afterward, forcing your body to start burning fat. At first, it is reluctant to do so, because you have to convince it that you really are starving, but once it does, you will have lots of energy on demand. To eliminate the need for transportation, you need to cover significant distances on foot, carrying loads, until your body adjusts by developing denser bone, thicker cartilage, stronger muscles and a more powerful cardiovascular system.

Mind you, there is nothing wrong with comforts, and even with luxuries. Bicycling is better than walking. Collecting rainwater and using a solar water heater for showers is better than going around smelling like a goat. A solar panel and a battery are an excellent idea if you like to read before bedtime. What is important is that these things be treated as luxuries rather than necessities, because then their sudden disappearance will not come as a shock. Moreover, each of these luxuries can become an encumbrance if the situation calls for a sudden change of plans and you cannot function without them. And you will need to function — if only to provide comforts to those around you who cannot function without them.

Surviving Radical Cashectomy

It seems inevitable that large parts of the population, including those that currently consider themselves middle class, will become penniless well before money becomes useless and therefore unimportant. Those who have debt will find it harder and harder to make the payments. Those who own property will find it harder and harder to afford the property taxes and the municipal fees. The money system will take an ever-increasing bite out of everything you do. But this is only true of economic relationships that are monetized — that have monetary value and involve the exchange of money. To reduce dependence on the money economy, everyone will be forced to invent ways to demonetize their lives and that of the people around them.

Savings and personal property can be transformed into the stock in trade of human relationships, which then give rise to reciprocal flows of gifts and favors — efficient, private and customized to personal needs. This requires a completely different mindset from that cultivated by the consumer society, which strives to standardize and reduce everything, including human relationships, to a client-server paradigm in which money flows in one direction while products and services flow in the opposite direction. Customer A gets the same thing as customer B, for the same price.

This is very inefficient from a personal perspective. Resources are squandered on new products whereas reused ones can work just as well. Everyone is forced to make do with mediocre, off-the-shelf products that are designed for planned obsolescence and do not suit them as well as ones crafted to meet their specific needs. A commodity product can be manufactured on the opposite side of the planet, whereas a custom one is likely to be made locally, providing work for you and the people in your community. But commodity products are also very efficient, from the point of view of extracting profits and concentrating wealth while depleting natural resources and destroying the environment. However, this is not the sort of efficiency you should be concerned with. It is not in your interest.

This, then, is the correct stance vis à vis the money economy: you should appear to have no money or significant possessions. But you should have access to resources, such as food, clothing, medicine, places to stay and work and even money. What you do with your money is up to you. For example, you can simply misplace it, the way squirrels do with nuts and acorns. Or you can convert it into communal property of one sort or another. You should avoid getting paid, but you should accept gifts and, of course, give gifts in return. You should never work for money, but always donate your time and effort charitably. You should have a minimum of personal possessions, but plenty to share with others. Developing such a stance is hard, but, once you do, life actually gets better. Moreover, by adopting such a stance, you become collapse-proof.

The Revised Playbook

People have been known to get along quite happily without written law, lawyers, courts or jails. Societies always evolve an idea of what is forbidden and find ways to punish those who transgress. In the absence of an official system of justice, people generally become much more careful around each other, because running afoul of someone may lead to a duel or give rise to a vendetta, and because, in the absence of jails, punishments tend to become draconian, coming to include dispossession, banishment and even death, which are all intended to deter and to neutralize rather than to punish.

The transition to a lower-energy system of jurisprudence will no doubt be quite tumultuous, but there is something we can be sure of: many laws will become unenforceable at its very outset. This development, given our definition of what is criminal, will de facto decriminalize many types of behavior, opening new, relatively safe avenues of legal behavior for multitudes of people, creating new opportunities for the wise and further tempting the evil and the foolish.

As a safety precaution, you might want to distance yourself from the legal system and, to the extent that this is possible, find your own justice. As an exercise, examine each of your relationships that is based on a contract, lease, deed, license, promissory note or other legal instrument and look for ways to replace it with a relationship based on trust, mutual respect and common interest. Think of ways to make these relationships work within the context of friendships and familial ties.

To protect yourself from getting savaged by the justice system as it degenerates into oppression, try to weave a thick web of informal interdependency all around you, where any conflict or disagreement can be extinguished by drawing in more and more interested parties, all of them eager to resolve it peaceably, and none of them willing to let it escalate beyond their midst. Struggle for impartiality when attempting to mediate disputes and be guided by your wisdom and your sense of justice rather than by laws, rules or precedents, which offer poor guidance in changing times.

Lowering Your Standards

Here are a few highlights from what amounts to a very large set of abnormal social standards. The pattern is a general one: when an abnormal society imposes and enforces a standard, there is a reasonable likelihood that the standard itself is part of the overall social pathology. It makes sense to re-examine what society considers important, and why. For example, Americans think it is important to have perfectly straight, shiny bluish-white teeth, and children are said to need orthodontic treatments. In other countries, ivory-colored teeth are considered normal for people and elephants alike, and crooked teeth are fine, provided they do not interfere with chewing food. Another example: Americans consider body odors and animal smells repulsive, but acrid, toxic chemical odors (be they from deodorants and disinfectants, engine exhaust or off-gassing plastics and synthetic fabrics) are just fine, although it is the latter that are likely to kill you by causing cancer. Finally: although gluttony still makes the list of mortal sins, in America it is quite permissible to be obese and people can let themselves go without being regarded as weak-willed. But there is no such special dispensation for abusers of substances other than food. Those who are not obese are considered "in shape" — that is, especially virtuous, thanks to some special diet coupled with an arduous exercise regimen. In the pantheon of American celebrities, there is no deity for a normal person to worship — a non-exercising non-gluttonous non-dieter — while exactly such people are the norm the world over.

American children from about age six up to the age of fourteen should properly be counted as part of the prison population. At best the prison is a minimum-security establishment, where children get day passes to engage in an approved set of activities, which nevertheless have to be supervised by properly authorized but underpaid and often undereducated adults. I was lucky to have grown up like children in much of the rest of the world, wandering around by myself as I pleased, roaming the countryside with other children, and was generally left alone much of the time. From about age eight, during the summer vacation, I was charged with doing most of the grocery shopping, which I often did on my bicycle, riding home with heavy sacks precariously balanced on the handlebar. By the time I was eleven, my parents thought nothing of taking a vacation without me, leaving me with the keys and some money. In the United States, they would have been ratted out by some supposedly helpful, concerned neighbor, charged with child neglect, and Child Protective Services would have rushed in to confiscate me and put me in a kiddy concentration camp, first medicating me into submission, then forcing me to eat junk food while watching countless hours of television. Of course, some American babies do need to be babysat their entire lives — but that's what the Secret Service is for. As for the rest of them, I wish them the best of luck in staying away from babysitters, Child Protective Services goons and nosy busybody neighbors, because they will certainly need it.

Sooner or later, we all have to die, and it is only a slight exaggeration to say that in America death is either a crime or a medical accident.

Of course, death is never one to ask permission of the courts or the doctors, but those who do death's bidding can easily find themselves charged with a crime or sued. Suicide is illegal, and the suicidal are considered insane and medicated until they become easy to control, no matter how watertight their reasons for wanting to end it all quickly. Helping someone commit suicide is also illegal. Dying in your own bed is almost impossible unless you do it in secret: anyone who finds out that you are dying and doesn't call an ambulance may end up in a lot of trouble. If you refuse or interfere with your own treatment, you are likely be deemed incompetent and restrained, sedated and forcibly treated.

What is not illegal is keeping people alive against their will and fashioning them into wired, intubated, ghastly science experiments. Doctors pride themselves on such incongruous achievements, and those who manage to extend their life beyond all odds are considered heroic. Many of the higher animals, humans among them, possess an instinct that tells them when they are near death. Following this instinct, they stop feeding, seek seclusion, become very still and await the inevitable end with dignified resignation. This innate behavior is denied to Americans, be they human or animal: they are not qualified to decide when it is time for them to die. This is a deep cultural flaw that affords the pathological fear of death the status of a heroic struggle.

This large set of abnormal social standards makes it perfectly normal to be highly suspicious of American officials or professionals who declare that something is required for reasons of safety, health or public order. But one must be very careful around them, lest they forcibly medicate you, dispossess you, imprison you or take away your children. Challenging them is like challenging your local insane asylum's Napoleon Bonaparte — with the added complication that he happens to be running the asylum. As the system that props them up decays and crumbles and their power wanes, they are likely to start grasping at straws, asserting their dominance in ever-more-controlling and forceful ways. Staying off their radar will require skill and imagination. But once this transition period is over, you will be able to set your own standards on how to be born, grow up, live and die, as mankind has done for millennia, and for this it is helpful to think ahead and discard most of the cultural garbage that has been foisted on you by some rather questionable authorities.

Playing the Part

When faced with economic collapse, national bankruptcy or outright failure of the entire social and political experiment, there doesn't seem to be a lot of scope for fruitful large-scale social collaboration. Gathering large segments of a collapsing society around you is unlikely to help you escape its fate. Adapting to a drastically new set of circumstances is a deeply personal matter, because the process of adaptation is highly individual and largely psychological and not something to be shallowly bantered about with strangers. As far as preparation, beyond a fairly small set of glaringly obvious steps, preparing for collapse in groups may be quite futile. The specific circumstances are impossible to predict and any sufficiently specific or realistic plan breaks down into minute details that are of little interest to anyone confronting even slightly different circumstances. Preparing in groups by following a single template may also turn out to be worse than futile, producing the unintended effect of putting more eggs in fewer baskets. Lastly, the effectiveness of any given trick is inversely proportional to the number of people who are aware of it and attempt to make use of it.

However, becoming a hermit is neither desirable nor possible for most of us. What public persona can we present that would not mire us in self-contradiction? How does one play the part of someone who is well-informed, not too frightened by the prospect of a future that does not resemble the past and wants to be prepared for it? My simple answer is that there is no role, no screenplay or storyboard or character. This is not to say that acting skills are useless. Quite the opposite — navigating through a disrupted time requires a higher than usual level of mimicry and outward conformism. A large proportion of the people you will encounter will be suffering and looking for someone to blame for their suffering — someone who is not one of "us." Beyond the important matter of personal safety, you will need to understand who has what you need and how to get it from them. Keep in mind that these people will most likely be too stressed to be interested in you, your opinions, knowledge or unique persona. They will be too busy trying to get what they need to survive. What they will want to see in you is a faithful and respectful reflection of themselves. If their minds are simple, then even a rough approximation will suffice to convince them that you are one of them, and that therefore they should help you rather than hurt you; but if you plan to plead your case before the subtle and the powerful, it may be helpful to brush up on Stanislavski's system of method acting. The best roles you will find will be cameos in other people's plays.

In a completely fascist country, the one remaining personal freedom is the freedom to look and act like a complete fascist. In a country that has been gradually slipping toward greater authoritarianism and ever-tighter social control, be it through increasing militarism, the criminal justice meat-grinder or any of the other, parallel trends, other freedoms may still exist, but their exercise is likely to become increasingly dangerous. Displays of extreme individualism, such as the public expression of non-mainstream political opinions, are bound to become quite risky. Taking such risks seems rather unnecessary, unless one wants to play the part of a martyr for a lost cause — and it is hard to see why anyone would want to play that role.

The Settled and the Nomadic

In the United States, there appear to be few ways to make the collapse scenario work out smoothly for oneself and one's family. The whole place seems too far gone in a particular, unsustainable direction. It is a real creative challenge and we should be giving it a lot of serious thought. Some of us are, and most often the flight of this thought alights on a singular existential question: Where to ensconce and secrete our precious selves, there to sit out the gathering storm? In a nation of nomads, who think nothing of growing up in one state, going to school in another and settling down in a third, it is surprising to see that so many people come to think that, during the most unsettled of times, some special place will sustain them perpetually. More likely than not, they will be forced to stay on the move.

Suppose you live in a big city, in an apartment or a condo. You depend on municipal services for survival. A week without electricity, or heat, or water, or gas or garbage removal spells extreme discomfort. Any two of these is a calamity. Any three is a disaster. Food comes from the supermarket, with help from the cash machine or the credit card slot at the checkout station. Clean clothes come from the laundromat, which requires electricity, water and natural gas. Once all the businesses have shut down and your apartment is cold, dark, smells like garbage (because it isn't being collected) and excrement (because the toilet doesn't flush), perhaps it is time to go camping and explore the great outdoors.

So let's consider the countryside. Suppose that you own a homestead and have a tiny fixed rate mortgage that shrivels to next to nothing after a good bout of inflation, or that you own it free and clear. If it's in a developed suburban subdivision, there will still be problems with taxes, code enforcement, psychopathic members of your local homeowners' association and other troubles, which could get worse as conditions deteriorate. Distressed municipalities may at first attempt to jack up rates to cover their costs instead of simply closing up shop. In a misguided effort to save property values, they may also attempt to enforce codes against such necessities as compost heaps, outhouses, chicken coops and crops planted on your front lawn. Keep in mind, also, that the pesticides and herbicides lavished on lawns and golf courses leave toxic residues. Perhaps the best thing to do with suburbia is to abandon it altogether.

A small farm offers somewhat better possibilities for growing food, but most farms in the US are mortgaged to the hilt, and most land that has been under intensive cultivation has been mercilessly bombarded with chemical fertilizers, herbicides and insecticides, making it an unhealthy place, inhabited by men with tiny sperm counts. Small farms tend to be lonely places, and many, without access to diesel or gasoline, would become dangerously remote. You will need neighbors to barter with, to help you and to keep you company. Even a small farm is probably overkill in terms of the amount of farmland available, because without the ability to get crops to market or a functioning cash economy in which to sell them, there is no reason to grow a large surplus of food. Tens of acres are a waste when all you need is a few thousand square feet. Many Russian families managed to survive with the help of a standard garden plot of one sotka, which is 100 square meters, or, if you prefer, 0.024710538 acres or 1076.391 square feet.

The best place to settle down seems to be a small town or village: a relatively small, dense settlement, with about an acre of farmland for every thirty or so people, and with zoning regulations designed for fair use and sustainability, not opportunities for capital investment, growth, increased property values or other sorts of "development." Further, it will have to be a place where people know each other and are willing to help each other — a real community. There may still be a few hundred communities like that tucked away here and there in the poorer counties in the United States, but there are not enough of them, and most of them are too poor to absorb a significant population of economic migrants.

It is risky to stay put and depend on a small annual crop of staples to keep you alive, because climate upheaval is likely to produce crop failures, wreaking havoc with even the best-laid local plans for ensuring food security. Successfully defending one's turf against bandits requires weapons, training and an effective organization for maintaining patrols and watches, and the tiny society locked up inside its fortress walls may fall victim to its own siege mentality, cutting itself off from the world and degenerating into group psychosis. Those with varied interests and skills are unlikely to find ample scope for them in a small, landlocked community and become despondent and depressed. In tough times, the locals have a tendency to get ornery and reject newcomers, making it difficult to settle either within or anywhere near an established community.

And so it turns out that there may be plenty of places to visit, but there may not be a single place to go and stay. Like digging a grave, sitting down next to it and waiting for a nice passerby to tip you in when the time comes, the quest for a final abode as preparation for an uncertain time seems somewhat quixotic. We may be enticed by the call to regain the Garden of Eden, to build a new Jerusalem or simply to escape to a rustic cabin in the wilderness, leaving all evil and corruption behind. But, as a practical matter, once there, we will quickly find reasons to move on, or at least to take a vacation.

Having a permanent base of operations is certainly a good thing but, if so, then having two or three is even better. An itinerant lifestyle that cycles through them has many advantages. No matter how ornery the natives get, they will always welcome a familiar visitor who has something to offer: a few luxury items, stories of the outside world, spare parts and the know-how to maintain decrepit mechanical systems, or magic elixirs to calm, soothe and de-worm. The nomad is likely to develop heightened situational awareness and an acute sense of danger, and flee before deteriorating circumstances instead of becoming trapped by them. A settled community may quickly deplete every resource within a day's walk, but nomads can glean and gather what they need as they move, surviving off a much poorer environment. At a minimum, it makes sense to maintain at least a winter camp and a summer camp, because the needs and opportunities of each season are often very different. Summer is the time for spending time outside, ranging widely, gathering in the temporary bounty of nature and storing it for future use. Winter is the time for staying put, for safeguarding and consuming reserves and for mending things, while hiding from inclement weather.

Without fossil fuel-based transportation, travel will revert to its ancient, organic forms. People will move over unpaved footpaths or navigable waterways. When traveling on foot, they will use pack animals such as mules or donkeys to carry provisions, letting them graze along the way. Water transportation will once again rely primarily on sailboats, rowboats and, along canals and slow-moving rivers, barges pulled by either draft animals or people. In colder climates, frozen waterways will provide a perfectly level and virtually frictionless surface, making for a particularly efficient form of seasonal transportation.

Since settled communities are always suspicious of nomads, it is best to never let on that you are one. If your itinerary ranges between point A and point B, then it should be perfectly obvious to the people at point A that you are a permanent resident at point B, and vice versa. Settled people often have trouble imagining what it would be like to live as a nomad, and so it is best not to tax their imagination, to avoid provoking a fit of xenophobia. On the other hand, settled people feel an instinctual pang of sympathy toward anyone who is trying to find their way home. To seek out that sympathy in strangers, you need to have a place you call home, even if that place only exists in the past, in your imagination or wrapped in a rag at the bottom of your kit bag.

In a world where old systems are breaking down and old patterns of behavior no longer apply, discovering a good place to stay is likely to be the result of a happy accident rather than careful planning. And until such an accident occurs, the best plan is to keep moving.

Career Opportunities

IT MAY SEEM THAT A POST-COLLAPSE economic environment would not be conducive to thinking productively about concepts such as career and success. Or would it? Under normal circumstances, during a typical day in the USA, most people are struggling to keep their heads above water financially, while a tiny minority of already wealthy individuals becomes even richer. After the collapse occurs, most people will have no hope of holding it together. The fabulously rich will surely be in for a rocky ride as well, as their investments plummet in value, their property is looted and it becomes harder and harder for them to keep the distance between their precious persons and the tide of the great unwashed lapping at their front lawns.

But there is sure to be a third category — those who, by dint of being in the right place at the right time, unexpectedly end up with all the loot. These are people who have direct access to actual, physical resources: stockpiles of supplies or access to facilities that can provide a safe harbor, sustenance, transportation or medical aid. Their main concern will be with making sure that their hoard is not exposed: in insecure circumstances, obscurity becomes the better part of security. And there will certainly be a larger, fourth category — those who have skills that many people need and the foresight to equip themselves for practicing them without relying on the continued existence of an economy. This could be a carpenter who has the foresight to invest in a good set of traditional hand tools (electric-powered tools will be of limited use) or a pharmacist with the foresight to take his stock home right before his pharmacy is looted, or an obstetrician who is brave enough to start moonlighting as a midwife. Lastly, a great many people would prefer to retain a profession, even if it no longer provides gainful employment. Post-collapse, a medical marketing expert becomes an ex-medical marketing expert turned professional ditch-digger, while an expert on early 19th-century French romanticism remains able to find perfect felicity in sharing specialized knowledge, even if necessity intrudes on it with episodes of tiresome freelance ditch-digging. Some professions are only viable in the context of a functioning economy and therefore transitory. Others are of little economic value to start with and, having little to lose, are sometimes spared the worst ravages of collapse.

Clearly, many professions will not hold much promise in a post-collapse environment. For example, the demand for lawyers, plastic surgeons, psychiatrists, fashion consultants and financial advisers will drop, because ever fewer middle-class people will require or be able to afford their services. Likewise, jobs in sales and marketing are likely to dwindle. Other professions, such as repo-men, auctioneers and undertakers, will still be very much in demand, for a time. Whether or not you decide to switch professions, you should choose something lucrative, work hard for a while, stock up on what you need to start living sustainably and get out. There is no sense in diving into murky waters except to make a bundle, and it is risky to expose your wealth should you manage to accumulate any. Endlessly running on a financial treadmill, as so many people do today, will no longer be a viable option.

Asset Stripping

Russia's post-collapse economy was for a time dominated by one type of wholesale business: asset stripping. To put it in an American setting: suppose you have title, or otherwise unhindered access, to an entire suburban subdivision, which is no longer accessible by transportation, either public or private, too far to reach by bicycle and is generally no longer suitable for its intended purpose of housing and accumulating equity for fully employed commuters who used to shop at the now defunct nearby mall. After the mortgages are foreclosed and the properties repossessed, what more is there to do, except board it all up and let it rot? Well, what has been developed can be just as easily undeveloped.

What you do is strip it of anything valuable or reusable, and either sell or stockpile the materials. Pull the copper out of the streets and the walls. Haul away the curbstones and the utility poles. Take down the vinyl siding. Pull out the fiberglass insulation. The fancy bathroom fixtures can surely find a new use somewhere else, especially if new ones are no longer being imported due to lack of international credit.

Having bits of the landscape disappear can be a rude surprise. One summer I arrived in St. Petersburg and found that a new scourge had descended on the land while I had been away: a lot of manhole covers were mysteriously missing. Nobody knew where they went or who had profited from their removal. One guess was that the municipal workers, who had not been paid in months, took them home with them, to be returned once they got paid. The manhole covers did eventually reappear, so there may be some truth to this theory. With the gaping manholes positioned throughout the city like so many anteater traps for cars, you had the choice of driving either very slowly and carefully, avoiding each one, or very fast, betting your life on the proper functioning of your shock absorbers.

Post-collapse Russia's housing stock stayed largely intact, but an orgy of asset stripping of a different kind took place: not just leftover inventory, but entire factories were stripped down and exported. What went on in Russia under the guise of privatization is a subject for a different book, but whether one refers to it as "privatization" or "liquidation" or "theft" doesn't matter: those with title to something that is worthless for its intended use will still find a way to extract value from it, making it even more worthless. An abandoned suburban subdivision might be worthless as housing, but it may still be valuable as a dump site for toxic waste.

Just because the economy is going to collapse in the most heavily oil-addicted country on earth doesn't necessarily mean that things will be just as bad everywhere else. As the Soviet example shows, if the entire country is for sale, buyers will materialize out of nowhere, crate it up and haul it away. First they will export the high-value items: furnishings, equipment, works of art, antiques. The last remnant of industrial activity is usually the scrap iron business. There seems to be no limit to the amount of iron that can be extracted from a mature post-industrial site using manual labor.

Drugs and Alcohol

A rather striking similarity between Russians and Americans is their propensity to self-medicate. While the Russian has traditionally been single-heartedly dedicated to the pursuit of vodka, the American is more likely than not to have also tried cannabis. Cocaine has also had a big effect on American culture, as have opiates. There are differences as well: the Russian is somewhat less likely to drink alone or to be apprehended for drinking, or being drunk, in public. To a Russian, being drunk is almost a sacred right; to an American, it is a guilty pleasure. Many of the unhappier Americans are forced by their circumstances to drink and drive; this does not make them, nor the other drivers, nor the pedestrians (should any still exist) any happier.

The Russian can get furiously drunk in public, stagger about singing patriotic songs, fall into a snow bank, and either freeze to death or be carted off to a drunk tank. All this produces little or no remorse in him. Based on my reading of H. L. Mencken, America was also once upon a time a land of happy drunks, where a whiskey bottle would be passed around the courtroom at the start of the proceedings and a drunken jury would later render a drunken verdict. But Prohibition ruined all that. Russia's prohibition lasted only a few short years, when Gorbachev tried to save the nation from itself and failed miserably.

When the economy collapses, hard-drinking people everywhere find all the more reason to get drunk, but much less wherewithal with which to procure drink. In Russia, innovative market-based solutions were quickly improvised, which it was my privilege to observe. It was summer, and I was on an *elecktrichka* — a local electric train — heading out of St. Petersburg. It was packed, so I stood in the vestibule of the car and gazed at rainbows (it had just rained) through the missing windowpane. Soon, activity within the vestibule caught my attention.

At each stop, grannies with jugs of moonshine would approach the car door and offer a sniff to the eager customers waiting inside. Price and quality were quickly discussed, an agreed-upon quantity was dispensed in exchange for a fistful of rubles, jug to mug, and the train moved on. The atmosphere was tense, because along with the paying customers there came many others, who were simply along for the ride, but expected their fair share nevertheless. I was forced to make a hasty exit and jam myself into the salon, because the freeloaders thought I was taking up valuable freeloading space.

There might be a few moonshine-makers left in rural parts of the United States, but most of the country seems to be addicted to cans and bottles of beer, or jugs, plastic or glass, of liquor. When this source dries up due to problems with interstate trucking, local breweries will no doubt continue to operate, and even expand production, to cope with both old and new demand, but there will still be plenty of room for improvisation. I would also expect cannabis to become even more widespread; it makes people less prone to violence than liquor, which is good, but it also stimulates their appetite, which is bad if there isn't a lot of food. Still, it is much cheaper to produce than alcohol, which requires either grain or another source of sugar, or natural gas and complicated chemistry.

In all, we should expect drugs and alcohol to become one of the largest short-term post-collapse entrepreneurial opportunities in the United States, along with asset stripping and security.

Providing Security

Security in the post-collapse Soviet Union was, shall we say, lax. I came through unscathed, but I know quite a few people who did not. A childhood friend of mine and her son were killed in their apartment over the measly sum of one hundred dollars. An elderly lady I know was knocked out and had her jaw broken by a burglar who waited outside her door for her to come home, assaulted her, took her keys and looted her place. There is an infinite supply of stories of this sort.

Empires are held together through violence or the threat of violence. Both the US and Russia were, and are, serviced by a legion of servants whose expertise is in using violence: soldiers, policemen, prison wardens and private security consultants. Both countries have a surplus of battle-hardened men who have killed, who are psychologically damaged by the experience, and have no qualms about taking human life. In both countries, there are many, many people whose stock in trade is their use of violence, in offense or defense. No matter what else happens, they will be employed or self-employed; preferably the former.

In a post-collapse situation, all of these violent men automatically fall into the general category of private security consultants. They have a way of creating enough work to keep their entire tribe busy: if you don't hire them, they will still do the work, but against you rather than for you. Rackets of various sizes and shapes proliferate, and, if you have some property to protect, or wish to get something done, a great deal of your time and energy becomes absorbed by the effort to keep your private security organization happy and effective. To round out the violent part of the population, there are also plenty of criminals. As their sentences expire, or as jail overcrowding and lack of resources force the authorities to grant amnesties, they are released into the wild and return to a life of violent crime. But now there is nobody to lock them up again because the machinery of law enforcement has broken down due to lack of funds. This further exacerbates the need for private security and puts those who cannot afford it at additional risk.

There is a continuum of sorts between those who can provide security and mere thugs. Those who can provide security also tend to know how to either employ or otherwise dispose of mere thugs. Thus, from the point of view of an uneducated security client, it is very important to work with an organization rather than with individuals. The need for security is huge: with a large number of desperate people about, anything that is not looked after will be stolen. The scope of security-related activities is also huge: from sleepless grannies who sit in watch over the cucumber patch to bicycle parking lot attendants and housesitters, all the way to armed convoys and snipers on rooftops.

As the government, with its policing and law enforcement functions, atrophies, private, improvised security measures cover the gap it leaves behind. In Russia, there was a period of years during which the police were basically not functioning: they had no equipment, no budget, and their salaries were not sufficient for survival. Murders went unsolved, muggings and burglaries were not even investigated. The police could only survive through graft. There was a substantial amount of melding between the police and organized crime. As the economy came back it all got sorted out, to some extent. Where there is no reason to expect the economy to ever come back, one must learn how to make strange new friends, and keep them, for life.

The scope for security operations is virtually unlimited: as the populace becomes increasingly distressed economically, all items of value will need to be kept out of view or carefully guarded — preferably both. The first requirement in any middling-to-large transaction will be to provide security. An organization that can provide security in an unstable environment is thus well-positioned to branch out into a multitude of other services: warehousing, logistics, transportation, finance and legal services.

Serving Your Country

If you find that you need to switch professions, and want to remain within the official economy, then you may decide to transition into the area of government contracting, availing yourself of the ample opportunities presented by official corruption, graft and politically sanctioned organized crime, which are sure to continue seeing substantial growth. There will be a great deal of government inventory of all sorts — from very expensive weapons systems to very expensive toilet seats — to be sold off, sometimes at a substantial profit. If you have a flair for international deal making, then finding foreign buyers for liquidated US government assets might be something you could ease your way into.

Although government work may be steady for a time, it also involves following rules and regulations (or at least pretending to), toeing the line, turning a blind eye and playing the politics. Also, it rarely provides the satisfaction of getting something useful accomplished. Finally, unless you manage to position yourself close to the top of the food chain, where billions in public money regularly go missing with hardly any questions asked, it is never going to be particularly lucrative. Profiting from government corruption is a high-stakes game, with only the extremely well connected admitted to the table.

One area of government employment to avoid is in the federal intelligence and security agencies, because they are much too silly. Compared to the Soviet Union's KGB, which was known for the high quality of its staff and its fearsome competence, the bumbling American intelligence and security services have never measured up. During the Cold War, one of their main activities was exaggerating the Soviet threat through fanciful interpretation of scarce and ambiguous data, in order to justify their own budgets, as well as those of their colleagues in national defense. One Soviet deserter I spoke with, who at the time worked as a consultant for the CIA, privately characterized it as "a very silly organization." It may be that the people he consulted for — Kremlinologists, the ones who failed to predict the Soviet collapse — are a bit sillier than the others, but overall, the common image is of a politicized, bumbling, sprawling and ineffectual bureaucracy. The attacks of September 11, 2001, which it also failed to detect, prevent or even adequately understand afterward, were a palpable hit to its reputation, and although terrorism is not a major source of mortality in the US (it would take a 9/11-sized attack almost every month for it to rival the homicide rate) the response was a sort of desperate hypertrophy of the American security apparatus. It is getting bigger and more invasive all the time, but there are few signs that it is getting any smarter, and its growth is starting to look like the final feeding frenzy of a fatally wounded beast. While members of the KGB went on to play a big role in Russia's post-collapse government, because they were competent and well organized, no such happy end seems likely for the hapless American spooks. Once the air starts leaking out of the federal budget, their fortunes will deflate along with it.

Alternative Medicine

Black market medicine promises to be particularly interesting, although perhaps not particularly lucrative. The cash economy will inevitably come to include pharmaceuticals, which in the United States are overpriced and often not available over the counter, but which can be manufactured in underground laboratories or purchased elsewhere in the world and imported in bulk. In addition, every year there are more and more people for whom Western medicine does not work, or works badly, and who are learning to avail themselves of the pharmacopeia of traditional medicine. Although there are some exotic ingredients used in traditional medicine, many medicinal herbs can be grown in most places, do not require complex cultivation and are, in fact, weeds. Once Western medicine and the pharmaceutical industry on which it depends enter a period of decline, it is likely that acceptance of traditional medicine will increase.

If black market pharmaceuticals may be somewhat lucrative, then what about black market medical practice? At some point it will come to include office visits and even surgery that are at first administered as "free care," but if one wants a follow-up visit, then one would have to offer a "gift." Currently, doctors in the US are sandwiched between layers of lawyers, insurance companies and pharmaceutical companies, all of whom require a profit in order to exist. Once there is no profit to be made by anyone, only the doctors will remain, because they (and nurses) are the only ones who are indispensable to the practice of medicine. They will once again start making house calls and work for whatever they can get: a bit of cash or even food, or simply because they care about their patients and want to be helpful and respected. They would be well advised to become competent herbalists before their pharmaceutical supply dries up.

Alternative Transportation

When I was in St. Petersburg in the summer of 1990, the lives of drivers were complicated by gasoline shortages, which resulted in long lines at the few gas stations that happened to be open, often made worse by a ten-liter limit on gasoline purchases. For many drivers, this meant that many hours had to be spent looking for gas. Some knew how to buy gasoline on the black market, through the various government depots that received their allotments separately from the retail distribution system, but there they had to pay black market prices. What was a headache for drivers turned out to be a bonanza for non-drivers: almost every private car was for hire, in a manner of speaking. To get a lift, all I had to do was stand by the side of the road and stretch out my hand. Within minutes, a car would pull over. The driver would ask me where I wanted to go, and answer Yes or No. There was rarely room for negotiation: either it was along his way, or it was not. The driver would also name the price — usually two or three rubles — which was most reasonable. A couple of years later, the gasoline situation improved and I could have stood by the side of the road with my hand out all day, if I wanted to, and be in no danger of getting anywhere.

Standing by the side of the road all day with your hand out describes the situation we should expect to see in the United States once gasoline shortages set in. Without a private car, it seems more difficult to get around in the US than just about anywhere in the world: there is little to no public transportation and little help from the people either. This was not always the case: just two decades ago, it was still quite possible to hitchhike across the country. As more and more people find themselves stranded by gasoline shortages, hitchhiking is likely to see a rebirth, along with a variety of jitney services. There are certainly efficiencies to be gained by having passengers stand rather than sit, packing people shoulder to shoulder in the beds of pickup trucks. The Cubans have done quite well using flatbed trucks to transport bicyclists across Havana. There is little doubt that countless similar solutions can be improvised; the challenge lies in suspending commercial regulations and public safety laws, and in muzzling the lawyers to prevent litigation in case of accident. Unsafe transportation is better than none at all.

Many people still enjoy flying, in spite of the constant stream of horror stories about passengers detained and searched without reason, possessions confiscated, jets full of passengers left stranded on the tarmac for days, and days and nights spent in airports whenever the weather turns inclement. The more or less constant stream of terror alerts focusing on airlines results in ever-more-onerous public safety measures at airports. The notorious shoe bomber and underwear bomber were taking steps in a particular direction, making it just a matter of time before another ideologically confused nobody decides to parlay an airline ticket into a lifetime of room and board care of the American taxpayer and takes the obvious next step, flying with a bomb up his rectum — or even just pretending to, interrupting the in-flight entertainment with loud cries of "Blimey, I fink I got a bomb up me bum!" After that, it will be body cavity searches for everyone, to be performed by some eager high school dropouts whom Homeland

Security will recruit and train. Once upon a time, flying was only for the bravest among us, and it is becoming that way again.

For those who do not want to drive or to fly, it is still possible to get around quite a bit of the country by train. Here, however, we find a system so neglected that trains on even the popular runs such as the Northeast Corridor are slow and unreliable. Attempts to breathe new life into the rail system, such as the Acela high-speed train, have run into problems with antiquated track, Byzantine organization and an ancient piece of legislation that compelled the engineers to design Acela to be the heaviest high-speed train in the world.

Even without fuel shortages, which are sure to come, America's transportation infrastructure is already in a bad way. It is bound to continue getting worse. For those who still want to travel, what alternatives are there? Aside from the truly exotic ones (hot air balloons, etc.) there are just two options that are widely available, reasonably safe, practical and enjoyable: sailing and bicycling. The two work well in combination. Sailboats can carry bicycles (with some difficulty: they need to be disassembled, placed in waterproof bags, and lashed to the lifelines). A sailboat's range is unlimited, and it can often carry many months' worth of provisions. Bicycles are perfect for inland forays up to a few hundred miles in search of more provisions.

If you believe that sailboats are luxury items, accessible only to the well-to-do, just check the foreclosure listings for them. You will find that a few months' rent will buy you a new, floating, rent-free home. If the cost is still too much, all you have to do is wait: the sailboat market is going from bad to worse. Once afloat, you will find that people on the water are almost invariably nice to each other and that there is no such thing as "waterway rage." There is also safety in numbers: both sailors and bicyclists tend to look out for each other. Having a moat around you provides a remarkable amount of both privacy and security: even if you're just yards away from shore, you might as well be in another world to anyone without a boat.

Social Work in the Home

In the ripe-for-collapse service economy, in the more prosperous places and for the more prosperous people, life can resemble an extended stay at an all-included resort or aboard a cruise ship. It is really quite amazing how many different types of service you can obtain, just walking or, more often, driving down a single street and waving a piece of plastic in every place you enter. Starting with breakfast, you can walk into a mom and pop diner (there are probably one or two left) and get your eggs done the way you like. Next, you can get a shave and a haircut, perhaps even a pedicure. After that, for whatever little thing that ails you, you have a choice of a chiropractor, shiatsu massage, acupuncture or Chinese herbs. With the onset of cocktail hour, someone will be on hand to serve you a drink.

And that is if everything is OK. Should you suddenly experience some serious problem, a number of other professionals will be on hand to assist you: the police, emergency room staff and a variety of counselors and therapists to assist with your rehabilitation. Once you are fully rehabilitated, it will be back to the pedicures, the massages and the cocktails. At no point would you need to ask anyone to do you any favors: it is their job to help you! Your friends might hear about your negative experiences, but at no point would you need to inconvenience them by actually asking for help. They would, of course, show concern; after all, what are friends for?

In an environment where most of one's needs are addressed by readily available, standardized product-service offerings, actual human relationships become a luxury, reserved for sex and fun. Even traditionally private, face-to-face functions, such as procreation and child rearing, can easily be taken care of by fertility clinics and child care centers. Many people spend most of their free time alone, having few close friends and a random, revolving collection of casual acquaintances. Deprived of any vital purpose, their interactions tend to become shallow and scripted, focusing on artificial subjects such as politics, sports events or business and technology. Successfully socialized individuals tend to favor simple, easy-to-read, overwhelmingly positive emotions and tend to avoid complex, nuanced or dark feelings or thoughts, for fear that these would negatively impact their inclusive fitness, perhaps causing them to be seen as troubled, and therefore in need of professional intervention.

Service economies are a rather recent invention. It was previously thought that value was created by taking various kinds of raw materials and transforming them into useful artifacts by the application of energy and skilled labor. This approach works, but creates a problem for the capitalists: once consumers have obtained everything they need, they no longer have to work as hard. When that happens, economic growth slows down or even stops, resulting in fewer opportunities to productively reinvest capital in further production. Capital — the accumulated profits from previous production — is worthless unless it can be used to charge interest via loans or to secure a share of future profits via direct investment in more production. Tricks such as planned obsolescence and the production of ever more short-lived, increasingly shoddy products are helpful here, but the real solution is to repackage products as services, allowing those holding the capital to collect rent. It has been found that the demand for services is far less flexible than the demand for products. For example, a consumer is more likely to defer the purchase of a new television set than to suspend her cable television service.

Although it is often thought that a service economy produces value, as an empirical matter it can be observed that what it produces in the United States is debt. One borrows money in order to provide and to receive services. Loans are extended based on the expectation that, in the future, demand for these services will be even higher, driving further economic growth. However, this is not a closed system: the delivery of these services is linked to external energy flows. Greater flows of energy, in the form of increased oil and natural gas imports, increased coal production and so forth, are failing to occur, for a variety of geological and geopolitical reasons. There is every reason to expect that the ability to deliver services will suffer as a result of energy shortages, collapsing the debt pyramid. The day is coming when you will walk into an establishment waving a piece of plastic, and nobody is particularly impressed with it and eager to serve you.

Now imagine a sudden transition to a world where it is nobody's job to serve or assist you. At first, we should expect bewilderment, accompanied by unprecedented levels of verbal and physical abuse, as those with unmet needs attempt to assert their vestigial consumer rights. Alongside the communal violence, mayhem and looting, people will start picking each other out from the crowds and connecting on an entirely new level by accepting responsibility for each other, and for each others' needs. The needs, it will turn out, are of two complementary kinds: to be helped and to give help. In those who give help, the triggering of the altruistic instinct, or the return to a traditional sense of virtue, combined with the instant ego gratification of confirming one's usefulness, produces a powerful endorphin release, giving rise to a feeling of euphoria. In those who receive help that is freely given, a deep feeling of gratitude is created, which, if it is expressed and acknowledged graciously, creates a powerful bond, but which, if it is expressed awkwardly, or through clumsy attempts at instant reciprocation, or if it is expressed but goes unacknowledged, can easily give rise to mutual resentment.

In the aftermath of a society that strives to regiment, compartmentalize and, if possible, monetize all human interactions, the transition to a society where aid and comfort are given directly requires a thorough cultural transformation. While many will find it liberating to cast aside the straitjacket of their jobs and to give help directly, many others will find that they lack the social skills to function outside the commercial, client-server pattern. Those parts of the population that have recent or continuing experience with circumstances that have forced them to provide for their mutual welfare — recent immigrant groups, minorities and the poor — can perhaps provide the cultural seed stock to make this transformation possible.

Moving away from an environment where behavior is controlled by the implicit threat of violence or punishment from outside the group — be it imprisonment, other kinds of penalties or dismissal from one's job — to one where no such external disciplinary authority exists, is bound to raise the intensity of human relationships. The methods of control that evolve may be brutal or subtle, their evolution affected by myriad factors, and the society that results can run the gamut from one where hell is other people, to one where only the children ever need to be disciplined and even they more often than not by a mere shrug or a raised eyebrow.

The transition from a framework where services are rendered by strangers to one where needs are served by friends and acquaintances will bring more and more activities back into the home: the kitchen, the basement workshop, the back yard and the home office. For as long as the authorities attempt to maintain a stranglehold on professional activities — for instance, arresting foreign-trained and unlicensed medical practitioners who serve those who cannot afford official medicine — a lot of this activity will be driven underground. But it makes sense to start this transition early, avoiding and preventing complications with the authorities as needed. Eventually, the authorities' regulatory zeal will become tempered by their need to be fed, clothed and treated for their ailments, making it possible to bring these activities back into the open, without fearing reprisal. Some may even come to play a helpful role, for instance, by closing streets to traffic and helping to transform them into viable public spaces. But until that happens, life will have to continue in private, in seclusion, centered around the home.

That's no way to run a business!

Those who run a business — be it a small family business like a corner grocery, or a large family business like Walmart — have to contend with the fact that the combination of skyrocketing food and energy costs, rising medical costs, falling real estate values and stagnant wages is putting increasing numbers of their workers in financial, psychological and, eventually, physical distress. A distressed workforce can hardly be a productive workforce, and companies must do whatever it takes to make it physically possible for their employees to function. What can companies do to remedy this situation? The obvious step of increasing wages runs the risk of stimulating consumption and driving up resource use, and that, in a resource-constrained world, causes commodities to spike and the rest of the economy to crash. A better approach is to cut costs — not for the business, but for its employees.

Consider treating the company and its employees as an economic unit: a single household, with a common set of costs. These costs can be cut very effectively by trading off slightly higher company costs against significantly lower employee costs. Each additional dollar paid out in wages is taxed as income, trimming it by about a third. It is then spent in the retail chain, generating profits for retailers and service providers, some of which may be your competitors, trimming it by another half or more. This same dollar can be stretched much further if the company uses it to buy products wholesale and makes them available to its employees either free of charge or for a nominal fee.

Many families are struggling with rising food costs. To help them, the company commissary can provide not just breakfast and lunch, but take-home dinners for the entire family. Periodically, it can provide other take-home items such as frozen chickens purchased in bulk, fresh organic vegetables from local CSA (Community-Supported Agriculture) farms, or a basket of popular foodstuffs purchased wholesale and assembled in-house.

Many employees are finding that their daily commute is eating ever deeper into their budgets because of the increasing price of fuel. In many cases, their ability to relocate closer to work is complicated by the stagnant real estate market and the higher price of housing closer to population centers. Telecommuting can help, but is only feasible for certain types of work. Here, the company can help by providing dormitories close by, which would allow employees to commute every other day, or even just once a week. For the younger, single employees, this may allow them to avoid spending money on housing altogether.

There are numerous other ways that a company can use its vastly greater negotiating power to effect significant savings for its employees while incurring a comparatively small additional cost. Examples run from directly providing family medical care through a company clinic to providing vacation packages at cost by renting out an entire vacation resort at a lower, negotiated group rate.

But perhaps the greatest opportunities for cost reduction lie in areas where employees' own efforts can replace services or products they would otherwise be forced to purchase, be it taking care of their elderly relatives instead of putting them in assisted living, or spending time with their children instead of paying for day care, or growing their own food in a community garden instead of shopping at a supermarket. Here, the company has to be willing to accommodate shorter working hours, trading off the slightly lower efficiency of having more part-time employees against the resulting vastly greater efficiency of the company community when it is viewed as a single household.

There is no need to couch such initiatives in purely negative terms of cost containment. Here is how Eric Schmidt, CEO of Google, sees it: "The goal is to strip away everything that gets in our employees' way. We provide a standard package of fringe benefits, but on top of that are first-class dining facilities, gyms, laundry rooms, massage rooms, haircuts, car washes, dry cleaning, commuting buses — just about anything a hardworking employee engineer might want."

If you feel that such special treatment may be required for the pampered software artists at prosperous Google, but not for your own employees, then take a look at the long list of benefits enjoyed by the enlisted men and women of the US Air Force, which includes 30 days a year of paid vacation and unlimited free air travel. This is a fine example of making the best use of what you already happen to have to make a difference for your employees: if what you have is plenty of jet aircraft, then why not let your employees travel as much as they want?

Although the results of such efforts may at first be difficult to quantify, should they succeed, the resulting competitive advantage is likely to become obvious. Let your hard-nosed competitors try to run their businesses with distressed, disgruntled, overworked employees, while you reap the benefits of loyalty, solidarity and ésprit de corps. In due course, this should make your competitors attractive as acquisition targets.

One ready objection that this proposal normally encounters runs along the lines of, "If everybody did this, the economy would collapse." If it were implemented across the board, this would cut retailers and the government out of their share of your earnings, reduce both corporate profits and government expenditures, shrink the overall size of the economy, making it unable to sustain a large and growing national debt, and hasten economic collapse and national bankruptcy.

To which my response is: If everybody didn't do this, the result would be exactly the same. In fact, if you take a representative sample of America's CEOs you will find that their reaction to this proposal is tepid at best, and there is simply no question of "everybody doing this." Therefore you should feel free to do as you see fit, and rest assured that the collapse of the US economy will proceed apace, and that no one will be able to discern your fingerprints on any part of it.

The Permanently Unemployed Consumer

Developing and marketing products for a shrinking market poses an interesting set of challenges. Even if a company does an outstanding job and is able to steadily grow its market share, these gains are negated if the market itself continually shrinks by an ever-larger amount. For instance, a company might have an outstanding electric vehicle design, but it is destined to fall by the wayside during a period when the number of consumers that qualify for a car loan is trending downward, the used car market is glutted with repossessed vehicles, and federal, state and municipal governments are unable to upgrade their car fleets because their budgets are deep in the red.

Consumer product development tends to cater to individuals who live in houses or condos, have jobs to which they commute by car, and generate a steady stream of disposable income. This is the group to which the business press often refers collectively as "the consumer": one often reads that the consumer is retrenching, that the consumer's credit is tapped out, that the consumer's disposable income is shrinking and so on. The consumer is not growing. What is there left to do except design and manufacture fewer and fewer products?

The answer is as simple as it is surprising. The consumer is not melting away; the consumer is mutating and evolving. In the United States alone, half a million people a month (in round numbers) are being shed from the workforce. Although this is often portrayed as a temporary condition, job creation is not expected to pick up pace any time soon, and few people are willing to forecast when it will again exceed population growth. Even a rose-tinted economic scenario has to admit to a high probability of new energy price spikes triggering new recessionary periods, which would drive unemployment even higher.

Therefore, more often than not a job loss will set a person on a new career path, one that comes with a new set of challenges and options. Most significantly, these formerly employed people often no longer have sufficient income to afford the two items that dominate most household budgets — the house and the car, and all of the expenses associated with them. Medical expenses form a third category, and vary enormously depending on a person's age and medical condition, ranging from zero (for the healthy uninsured) to arbitrarily large (medical expenses being the largest single cause of personal bankruptcy).

Does permanent job loss mean that someone is no longer a consumer? In some cases the answer is Yes: some people continue to spend as if they still had a job, and the inevitable result is eventual destitution. Once they run out of unemployment benefits, savings and credit, their purchasing ability decreases to the barest minimum provided by food stamps. I don't mean to sound uncaring, but this does make them rather uninteresting from a new product marketing perspective.

But other people may be quick to shed their biggest categories of expense, walking away from their mortgage and their car loan, allowing their medical insurance to lapse, and developing a new lifestyle that is well within their new budgetary constraints. They may couch surf, take advantage of housesitting opportunities or rent a spot at a campground by the season. For the cold part of the year, they may head south and, again, camp out. They may look for seasonal employment, do odd jobs for cash, or use their skills to repair or make and sell items for cash.

With their largest expenses gone, their disposable income may actually be higher than it was before. However, their needs and requirements are quite different, and since most product offerings target the settled, fully employed consumer, they are already in many ways under-served. This is an area where new product development opportunities abound, and companies that gain a share of this growing market segment and build brand loyalty among this fast-growing consumer underclass will lock in a decade or more of profits and rapid growth. As a marketing strategy, it is not just recession-proof but actually recession-enhanced.

In saying that unemployed consumers are currently under-served, I do not mean to belittle the huge positive effect on their lifestyles that resulted from the recent major advances in mobile computing and communications. Laptops with wireless internet access have made it possible for a homeless person to run an internet business or a software company, manage an investment portfolio or contribute to an international scientific collaboration. Any of these things can now be done from an internet cafe or a public library or, in fine weather, even a bench in a city park or a tent at a campground. Cell phones make it possible to give radio interviews and participate in teleconferences from just about anywhere that is within sight of a cell phone tower. Hand-held GPS units allow people to find their way around and to retrieve items stashed in the woods via a precise set of coordinates.

But even here there is plenty of room for specific improvements: the umbilical cord of the laptop power supply and the cell phone charger hampers mobility. It would not be difficult to add small solar panels to the backs of cell phones and the lids of laptops, making it possible to recharge them simply by leaving them in the sun for an hour or two. Many people would be willing to trade off certain features, such as a high-powered microprocessor or a brilliant display, against lower power consumption and a reduced need to plug in.

In addition to such incremental improvements, certain completely new types of devices could be designed to serve some of the unique needs of the permanently unemployed. For example, it is not uncommon for them to be living in places that lack public utilities such as running water, making it impossible to use flush toilets. A commonsense adaptation is to put together a composting toilet, using a five-gallon drum and a toilet seat, with a length of dryer hose for the exhaust duct. A key component of this solution is the exhaust fan, which can be quite tiny and low-powered, but has to run continuously. A small computer fan connected to a lantern battery is adequate and lasts for many months, but an even better solution is a battery-backed exhaust fan powered by a solar panel that is designed to be installed in a partially opened window. Another example: a portable device that can detect the many environmental hazards that are likely to be present in such a less-than-ideal living environment; a combined smoke/carbon dioxide/carbon monoxide detector that can also detect toxins from burning synthetic materials would be perfect. A portable device for testing the safety of drinking water would also be very useful.

In addition to such new products, the permanently unemployed would also benefit from certain services designed to fit their unique needs. For example, a campground at which campsites are paired up with garden plots, allowing people to spend the summer months growing their own food, would suit people who have plenty of time, little money and nowhere to live. In cities, low-priced dormitories styled after Japanese capsule hotels with shower and locker facilities would make their lives much easier while also helping to improve sanitation and public health and preserve public order. There is a continuum between shelter and clothing, and the need to stay on the move has caused many people to seek shelter in dwellings that are not habitable in what amounts to indoor camping. There are as yet no products that specifically target this exciting new lifestyle.

We live in a time of steadily rising unemployment and, consequently, much emphasis is being placed on stimulating job creation. To this end, the federal government is continuing to throw money at a variety of infrastructure projects. An obvious question to ask is whether any of these projects have directly benefited the unemployed, beyond creating a few temporary jobs. It stands to reason that the jobs to create first are the ones in industries with the highest growth potential, where job creation can quickly become self-sustaining. As a matter of public policy, it would make perfect sense to provide seed money for what is certain to become a new high-growth industry segment: serving the needs of the permanently unemployed.

How (not to) to Organize a Community

Dire predictions made by authoritative figures can provide the impetus to attempt great things: establish community gardens and farmer's markets; lobby for improved public transportation, bike lanes and sidewalks; promote ride-sharing initiatives, weatherization of existing homes and more stringent construction standards for new ones, construction of windmill farms and installation of solar panels on public buildings, the use of composting toilets and high-efficiency lighting and so on. In the midst of all this organizational activity neighbors get a chance to meet, perhaps for the first time, and discover a commonality of interests that leads them to form acquaintances and perhaps even friendships. As they get to know each other, they start looking out for each other, improving safety and reducing crime. As the community becomes more tight-knit, it changes in atmosphere and appearance, becoming more fashionable and desirable, attracting better-educated and more prosperous residents while pricing out undesirable elements. News of these vast improvements spreads far and wide, and the community becomes a tourist mecca, complete with swank boutiques and pricy bric-à-brac shops and restaurants.

The undesirable elements are forced to decamp to a less desirable neighborhood nearby. There, they must endure high levels of crime, but are typically afraid to ask the police for help, having learned from experience that the police are more likely to harass them than to help them, to arrest them for minor offenses and round them up and deport them if they happen to be illegal immigrants. They also learn to be careful around members of local gangs and drug dealers. Since official jobs in the neighborhood are scarce, they seek informal, cash-based employment, contributing to an underground economy. Seeking safety in numbers, they self-organize along racial and ethnic lines, and, to promote their common interests, form ethnic mafias that strive to dominate one or more forms of illegal or semi-legal activity. Growing up in a dangerous, violent environment, their children become tough at a young age, and the ones that survive develop excellent situational awareness that allows them to steer clear of dangerous situations and to know when to resort to violence.

When the fossil fuel-based national economy shuts down due to the increasingly well-understood local ramifications of the global phenomenon of Peak Oil, both of these communities are harmed, but to different extents and in different ways. Some countries may continue to function for another decade or even longer: these are the countries that have enough oil of their own, as well as those that were far-sighted enough to enter into long-term barter agreements with the few remaining oil producers that still have a surplus of oil for export. But suppose that our two communities are in an English-speaking country, which is likely to be afflicted with the irrational belief that the free market can solve all problems on its own, even problems with the availability of critical supplies such as oil. Just as one would expect, the invisible hand of the market fails to make itself visible, but it is plain to see that fuel is no longer delivered to either of these communities (although in the second one some fuel is likely to still be available on the black market). Sooner or later, due to lack of supplies and maintenance at every level, the electricity goes off, water pumping stations cease to function, sewage backs up and makes bathrooms unusable, and garbage trucks no longer remove the garbage, which piles up, breeding rats, flies and cockroaches. As sanitary conditions deteriorate, diseases such as dysentery and typhoid reappear and spread. Since the medical system requires fuel for ambulances and running water, electricity, and oil-based pharmaceuticals and disposable supplies in order for hospitals and clinics to operate, none of which are now available, the surviving residents are left to care for each other as best they can and to bury their own dead. Along with the other municipal and government services, the police department ceases to function. Particularly important installations are guarded by soldiers or by private security, while the population is left to fend for themselves.

The effect on the two communities is markedly different. The first community is superficially better prepared, being better equipped for emergencies and perhaps even having laid in emergency supplies of food and water. But its prosperous nature makes a sudden transition to destitution and chaos much more of a shock. It also makes it a much more desirable target for looters. Used to living in safety and enjoying the protection of a benign and cooperative police department, the residents are not acculturated to the idea of countering violence with violence. Their response is more likely to take the form of a fruitless policy discussion rather than a spontaneous decision to go out and prophylactically bash some heads, causing the remaining heads to think twice. Unaccustomed to operating outside the law and having few connections with the criminal underworld, they are slow to penetrate the black market, which is now the only source of many necessary items, such as food, cooking fuel and medicines, including the ones previously looted from them. Worse yet, they once again become estranged from one another. Their acquaintances and friendships were formed within a peaceful, well-behaved, law-abiding mode of social behavior. When they are forced to turn to scavenging, outright theft and looting, prostitution, black market dealing, and consorting with criminals, they can no longer recognize in each other the people they knew before, and the laboriously synthesized community again dissolves into nuclear families. Where neighbors continue to work together, their ties are likely to be weak, based on altruistic conceptions of decency, mutual benefit, and personal sympathies — a far cry from the clear do-or-die imperatives of blood ties or clan or gang allegiance.

The second community is already accustomed to hardship and, not having quite so far to fall, can take the transition in stride. The prevalence of illegal activity prior to collapse smoothes the transition to a black market economy. Already resistant to the idea of relying on police protection, the residents are relieved when the police disappear from the streets, and a great deal of unofficial and illegal activity that previously had to be conducted in secret bursts out into the open. With the police no longer stirring the pot with their invasive arrests and confiscations, local criminal gangs now find themselves operating in a more stable environment and are able to carve up the neighborhood into universally recognized zones of influence, avoiding unnecessary bloodshed. The residents' children, already in the habit of roaming the streets in gangs and harassing and mugging strangers, now come to serve as the community's early warning system in case of an organized incursion. (Not that too many people would want to venture into such an area in any case, given its fearsome reputation.) Lastly, the prevalence of illegal drug dealing means that the neighborhood already has a trained cadre of black marketeers who can branch out into every other kind of commerce. Their ties to the international narcomafia, whose representatives tend to be well organized and heavily armed, provide numerous benefits, such as the ability to move people and contraband through the now highly porous national borders. If the narcomafia ties are sufficiently strong, a narcobaron may even take the community under his cartel's explicit protection, founding a new aristocracy to replace the now disgraced former ruling class.

Community organizing is quite wonderful, and can provide some of us with a perfectly pleasant way to while away our remaining happy days. But it does nothing to prepare us for collapse. A safe and congenial environment for you and your children is obviously very nice, much better than trying to survive among social predators. But the fewer the wolves the lamer, fatter and more numerous are the sheep. The central problem with community organizing is that the sort of community that stands a chance post-collapse is simply unacceptable pre-collapse: it is illegal, it is uncomfortable, and it is unsafe. No reasonable person would want any part of it. Perhaps the best one can do is to gather together all the unreasonable people, all the outcasts, misfits, eccentrics and sketchy characters with checkered pasts and nothing better to do. Give them an opportunity to provide for their own welfare and to keep themselves entertained. Keep the operation low-key and under the radar, and put up some plausible and benign public façade, or your nascent community will be shut down and dispersed. And if, through some indescribable process, all of these unreasonable people manage to amalgamate and self-organize into some sort of improvised community, then you win. Or maybe they win and you lose. Either way, you would deserve credit for attempting to do something unusual, something that might have actually worked.

There may be a few people who would be willing to tackle such an assignment. If they are serious about it, they will stay well hidden, and we will never know how many of them there were, or how many of them succeeded. As for the rest of us, who are itching to do something useful within the confines of the existing legal framework and economic reality, there is just one path: the path of emergency preparation, with the added twist that the emergency in question has to be accepted as permanent.

The first and obvious part of preparing for the permanent emergency is to construct systems that will allow some, ideally most, of the population to survive in the long run without access to transportation fuels, or to any of the technology that comes to a standstill when starved of transportation fuels. The second, equally important part involves laying in sufficient emergency supplies of food, medicine, cooking fuel, temporary shelter for displaced persons, and so on, to allow some, ideally most, of the population to survive in the short run, while the transition to non-fossil-fuel-based existence is taking place. Yet another task is to organize streamlined, military-style control structures that can step in to maintain order and provide security.

But the most important element of preparing for the permanent emergency is to devise a plan to force through a swift and thorough change of the rules by which society operates. Under emergency conditions, the current rules, laws and regulations will amount to a set of unachievable mandates and unreasonable restrictions. The existing way of changing the rules involves lobbying, deliberation, legislation, and litigation — time-consuming, expensive activities for which there will be neither the time nor the resources. There are no non-destructive ways to decomplexify complex systems, and the legal framework is one such system. By default, the procedure will be to universally ignore the old rules, but this is bound to cause mayhem and much loss of life. The best-case scenario is one in which the old rules are consigned to oblivion quickly and decisively. The public at large will not be the major impediment to making the necessary changes. Rather, it will be the vested interests at every level — the political class, the financial elite, professional associations, property and business owners, and, last but not least, the lawyers — who will try to block them at every turn. They will not release their grip on society voluntarily. There is just one institution with enough power to oppose them, and that is the US military. It would be most helpful if enough high-caliber military types with lots of stars on their epaulets could step up and lay down the new law: henceforth anyone who wants to litigate their orders will do so before a military tribunal. It is heartening to see that many of the world's militaries, the Pentagon included, have recently woken up to the reality of Peak Oil, and are taking steps to prepare for it, while our craven and feckless politicians and businessmen continue to wallow in denial. Clearly, many Americans would rather not live under military rule, but then beggars can't be choosers, and in any case, the alternative is bound to be even worse.

When taking part in community organizing activities, if your envisioned community is to survive the transition to a non-fossil-fuel-based existence, it is important to keep in mind a vital distinction: is this community going to operate under the old rules or the new rules? The old rules will not work, but the new ones might, depending on what they are. You might want to give the new rules some thought ahead of time, perhaps even test them out, as part of your community's permanent emergency preparation program.

In Conclusion

Since I have started writing articles on the subject of collapse, quite a few people have contacted me to tell me that, shocking as it may seem to them, basically they agree with me. This is, of course, heartening to hear, but what does it mean, really? All I've done is formulate a technique for comparing superpower collapses, and exploit it for all it is worth in a series of intentionally provocative thought experiments. I hope that agreeing with me is just a developmental stage of sorts, a resting point on the way from being in agreement with the country at large to grasping the sad truth about it and being in agreement with just a few close soul mates, if that. The big, rowdy party that was this country, with its lavish, garish, oversized, dominating ways, is nearing its end and soon the festive gathering will split up and people will wander home, each their own separate way. People like to party together but they like to nurse their hangovers alone.

Quite a few people have also written to ask me a question or two. "When is the collapse going to happen?" Well, I do not want the economy to collapse before everyone gets a chance to purchase this book, so let us hope for the best. "What do I plan to do?" Well, I am not sure. But I do wish to share this: I certainly do not plan to be trapped by any one plan. "What should I do?" Well, you should figure out what it is you absolutely need to lead a healthy, happy, fulfilling existence. Then figure out a way to continue getting it once the US economy collapses, taking a lot of society with it. (This is easier said than done; good luck!)

In this book, I have said some obvious things and some things that should surprise just about everyone. I have tried to express what many people think but fear to say, and perhaps even a few things that people fear to think. I have worked very hard to write a book on an important but seriously depressing subject that's nevertheless fun to read; I hope that I have succeeded. All that I ask in return is that you retain the ability to see things clearly, decide for yourself, and keep your sense of humor — no matter what happens.

I firmly believe that only an individual approach can bring something close to happiness. That is, ultimately, no one can know what is best for you and no one can prepare you for anything except you yourself. This, unfortunately, is impossible to do without feeling the pain of loneliness when things are not going so well. However, this pain does not have to be permanent: it also allows you to feel joy and satisfaction when the situation changes for the better. What many people forget is that most everyone feels pain in their lives. Although superficially it creates a feeling of separation from the rest of the world, it can also bring us closer together.

Index

corporations: collapse prevention
for, 129; food industry, 102–103;
judicial system and, 46–47; real
estate ownership, 76; staffing
structure, 86
crime, 47, 93, 151, 179
criminals, 48, 164
Cuba, 42, 106, 168
Czechoslovakia, 39
D
death, 151–152
debt, 2, 7, 64, 126, 148, 171
Deepwater Horizon oil spill, 36–37
defense. *See* military; security
democracy, 22, 58, 60, 126
democratic institutions, 58
denial, 7–10, 69
depression, 56, 107–108
development assistance loans, 59
diesel, 29, 69
diet, 29. *See also* food supply
diplomatic interventions, 43
disabilities, persons with, 92
disciplinary authorities, 173
discomfort, 147
disobedience, 113
disposable products, 96
dissidents, 46, 126, 144
divorce, 87
doctors, 167
drugs, 66, 105, 119, 162–163, 182.
See also pharmaceutical companies
E
Eastern Europe, 27, 44, 59
economists, 54, 55
economy: collapse of, 6–7, 10–11,
18–19, 54–55; confidence in,
54–55; dependence of, 6–7; effect
of ideology, 55–56; expectations
of collapse, 3–4; industrial, 57;
promoting development of, 59;
recovery in Soviet Union, 16–17;
recycling of, 65; service-based,
145, 169–173; underground, 180

education, 19, 56, 87, 109–114
elderly, 57, 89–90
election system, 58
electricity, 133
employment: alternatives to salaries,
101; effect of economic collapse,
82–87, 92; effect of for-profit
medicine, 107; middle-aged
workers, 84, 139, 146; reducing
dependence on money, 149;
skilled labor, 85, 159–160
energy. *See also* coal; gasoline;
natural gas; oil: imports, 18;
service delivery and, 171; in
Soviet Union, 68–69; supply
system, 68; in US, 69–75
enterprise software, 32, 35
EROEI (Energy Returned on
Energy Invested), 73
ethanol: effect on food supply,
99, 104; expectations for, 8; as
solution, 133
ethnic cleansing, 67
evictions, 75
evil empires, 22, 23, 50–52
Export Land Effect, 72
extinction, 120
F
factories, 161
families, 87–91
farming: comparison of, 28–30;
depopulation of districts, 24;
effect of biofuels, 133; kitchen
gardens, 85, 100–101, 102, 155;
small-scale, 104; Soviet history
of, 98–100; value of land, 93
fascism, 154
fast food, 102
federal intelligence agencies,
165–166
fertilizers, 29, 93, 99, 155
fiction, future as, 135–139
finances: comparison of, 19;
consumer goods and, 30;

About the Author

DMITRY ORLOV was born in Leningrad and immigrated to the United States at the age of 12. He was an eyewitness to the Soviet collapse over several extended visits to his Russian homeland between the late eighties and mid-nineties. He is an engineer who has worked in many fields, including high-energy Physics research, e-commerce and Internet security. Recently, Dmitry has been experimenting with off-grid living and renewable energy by giving up his house and car. Instead, he has been living on a sailboat, sailing it up and down the Eastern Seaboard, and commuting by bicycle. Dmitry believes that, given appropriate technology, we can greatly reduce personal resource consumption while remaining perfectly civilized.

For more about Dmitry and his work, visit cluborlov.com.

If you have enjoyed *Reinventing Collapse*, you might also enjoy other

BOOKS TO BUILD A NEW SOCIETY

Our books provide positive solutions for people who want to
make a difference. We specialize in:

**Sustainable Living • Green Building • Peak Oil
Renewable Energy • Environment & Economy
Natural Building & Appropriate Technology
Progressive Leadership • Resistance and Community
Educational & Parenting Resources**

New Society Publishers

ENVIRONMENTAL BENEFITS STATEMENT

New Society Publishers has chosen to produce this book on recycled paper made
with **100% post consumer waste,** processed chlorine free, and old growth free.

For every 5,000 books printed, New Society saves the following resources:[1]

21	Trees
1,911	Pounds of Solid Waste
2,103	Gallons of Water
2,742	Kilowatt Hours of Electricity
3,474	Pounds of Greenhouse Gases
15	Pounds of HAPs, VOCs, and AOX Combined
5	Cubic Yards of Landfill Space

[1]Environmental benefits are calculated based on research done by the Environmental Defense Fund
and other members of the Paper Task Force who study the environmental impacts of the paper
industry.

For a full list of NSP's titles, please call 1-800-567-6772 *or check out our website* at:

www.newsociety.com

NEW SOCIETY PUBLISHERS
Deep Green for over 30 years